WOOD IN THE LANDSCAPE

Materials in Landscape Architecture and Site Design

Rob W. Sovinski
Brick in the Landscape

Daniel M. Winterbottom
Wood in the Landscape

WOOD IN THE LANDSCAPE

*A Practical Guide to Specification
and Design*

Daniel M. Winterbottom, ASLA

JOHN WILEY & SONS, INC.

New York • Chichester • Weinheim • Brisbane • Singapore • Toronto

Library of Congress Cataloging-in-Publication Data:

Winterbottom, Daniel.
    Wood in the landscape : a practical guide to specification and design / Daniel Winterbottom.
        p.   cm. — (Materials in landscape architecture and site design)
    Includes bibliographical references (p.) and index.
    ISBN 0-471-29419-5 (cloth : alk. paper)
      1. Garden structures—Design and construction. 2. Landscape construction. 3.
    Carpentry. I. Title. II. Series.
    TH4961.W557 2000
    624—dc21   99-045536

Printed in the United States of America.

10 9 8 7 6 5 4 3 2 1

Dedicated to my parents,
Miriam Taleisnik and John Arthur Winterbottom,
who, through family hikes in the forest,
introduced me to the beauty of the trees,
and in crossing the timber bridges and passing the porches
filled with gingerbread ornamentation,
exposed me to the carpenter's craft

CONTENTS

ACKNOWLEDGMENTS

There are many people to thank who have given so much to make this book possible. To mention only a few is difficult, for those not included are certainly not forgotten. Much credit is due to Professor Linda Jewel, who, during my graduate studies, was one of the few people I knew who was interested in the fine crafts of landscape architecture. I was privileged to work with Linda, learn from her keen eye, and benefit from her commitment to students and her support of those of us venturing into the area of design technology. She was rare and truly inspirational. Since leaving the tools behind and working with students, the rewards have been great. The efforts of three of my students have made this work possible. Trent Thellan, whose early support was great, is responsible for much of the research. To Jodi Estes and Chad Wichers deep appreciation is due, for both not only achieved a high level of craft in their own work, but as artists provided great assistance with their illustrations. To my chair, Iain Robertson, who, despite his incredulous response when told about this project—"Why would anyone want to build of wood when stone will outlast us all?"—has been a wonderful colleague and has supported my efforts in full. I wish to thank Luanne Smith, who helped me create some of the projects included, William "Bill" MacElroy for his support over the years, and Niall Kirkwood, one of my few colleagues and friends who share a passion for design/technology as a legitimate field of interest. Thanks to Allan Robbins, Plastic Lumber Council; Butch Bernhardt, Western Woods; and Matt Sutton, ARCON/CSI. I am also grateful to the Johnson/Hastings Fund and Howard S. Wright Fund, the University of Washington, and the Graham Foundation for the

Arts and Humanities, and to the editors at John Wiley & Sons—Margaret Cummins, Jim Harper, and Maury Botton—who have been so supportive and helpful. Finally, none of this could have been done without the encouragement, editorial help, and love of my wife, Carol Bjork, who provided criticism, insight, and curiosity and made both the process and product a worthwhile and enjoyable journey.

WOOD IN THE LANDSCAPE

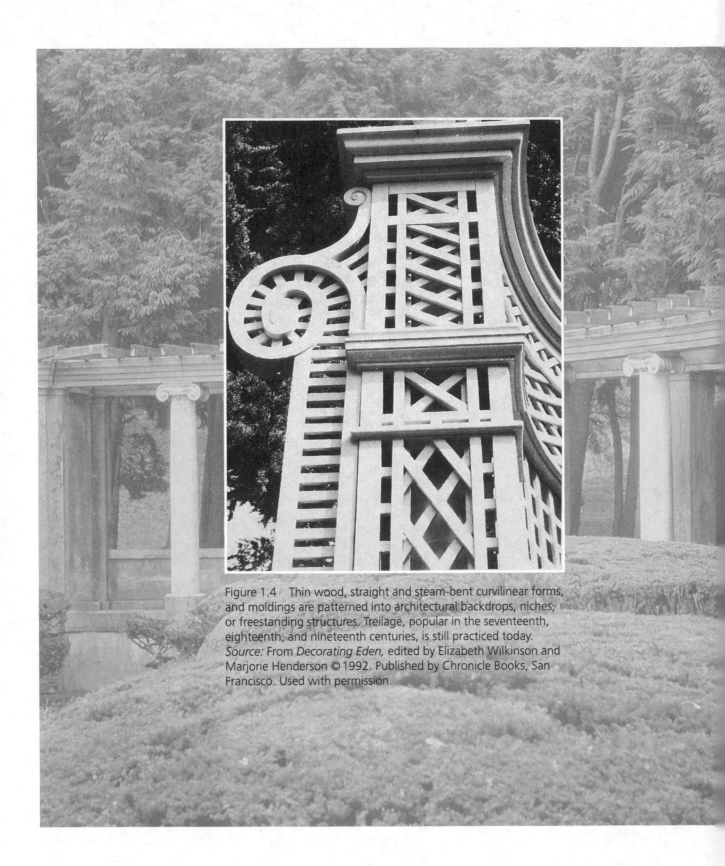

Figure 1.4   Thin wood, straight and steam-bent curvilinear forms, and moldings are patterned into architectural backdrops, niches, or freestanding structures. Treilage, popular in the seventeenth, eighteenth, and nineteenth centuries, is still practiced today.
Source: From *Decorating Eden,* edited by Elizabeth Wilkinson and Marjorie Henderson © 1992. Published by Chronicle Books, San Francisco. Used with permission.

1
INTRODUCTION

WOOD AS A BUILDING MATERIAL

This book stems from many years spent both in professional practice and in academia, teaching and researching the design and technology of landscape architecture at the University of Washington. In many ways the original impetus came when, as an apprentice to a local contractor at the age of 16, I arrived the first day at the job site and began framing my first roof. Shortly thereafter I fell in love with wood as a building material—its touch and smell, the visual qualities of the differing framing members—and over time I grew to appreciate its adaptability and range of uses. I learned most about wood as a building material "on the job" and through observing how different cultures used and expressed their individualism and traditions through wood structures. I saw how the wonderful rusticated pavilions of Calvert Vaux in New York's Central Park defined the sense of place (see Figure 1.7) and how the elaborate newel posts and individualistic detailing of New England fences, painted white to "fit in," allowed for the personal expression of the carpenter and at the same time spoke of the regional qualities of the built landscape, through form, color, and joinery. When I began my professional career as a landscape architect, and later as I taught courses on construction materials and methods at the university, I realized there were few resources available for both practitioners

3

and students that focused on wood as a building material for landscape architecture.

Shelves of books address the use of wood for architectural purposes, with general references on house construction, and, there are specialized works on post and beam construction, timber framing, roof framing, and window installations. In most engineering libraries there are hundreds of books providing structural calculations for the sizing of posts, beams, and trusses and calculations for the lateral and shear forces and the stresses of fastening mechanisms.

In my library searches I found few books specifically on the use of wood in the landscape. Many of the books I did find, although helpful, provide a general survey of all materials and construction methods and as such give only a cursory examination of specific materials. There are many books on garden structures, but the majority are simply illustrations of historic designs, with those fabricated of cast iron, stone, bronze, or wood thrown together and thus lacking an in-depth investigation on the subject of material detailing or, specifically, the craft of woodworking. Many books displayed at the hardware store checkout counter, including the Ortho series and others, contain pertinent information but are directed to the homeowner doing weekend projects and not to the serious student or practitioner creating structures in public parks, university campuses, and urban streetscapes. The purpose of this volume on wood construction, the second in a series of books on landscape architectural materials, is to bring a depth of focus and provide a valuable resource specifically designed for landscape architecture students and practitioners in the field.

The intent of *Wood in the Landscape* is to provide the relevant information needed by students and practitioners to knowledgeably design and appropriately detail with wood. This book provides sections on material qualities, fundamental design concepts, technical information on finishes and mechanical fasteners, and contemporary examples of built projects. In addition, the book presents new information on wood composition products and alternative materials that are environmentally friendly and offer options to the use of an increasingly expensive and rapidly declining resource—high-quality wood.

Wood in the Landscape serves not only as a technical manual, providing sizing charts, fastener selections, and so forth, but also investigates the multitude of design possibilities inherent in the material. Whether used in a natural form as in the art of rustication, or as a material to be carved or machined as in the Craftsman tradition, or as members in the complex puzzles of joinery as in the Japanese tradition, wood brings us back, at a subconscious and sensorial level, to the roots of our building heritage and back to the natural world. The different grains, colors, and expressions inherent in wood give it a warm, lively quality found in few other materials.

There are also many practical advantages to wood as a building material. Wood, in comparison with other building materials such as concrete or steel, is light in weight. In comparison with reinforced concrete and other materials, wood is generally very economical and as a building material relatively simple and clean to work with as both a framing and finishing material. Moreover, many components can be prefabricated and assembled in the field with a variety of techniques, each with its own character and unique expression. Wood is one of the most versatile building materials, offering a great range of forms—from curved glue-laminated structural members to elaborate moldings to fantastic carved relief pieces. Because wood is easy to cut and join, almost any building configuration can be achieved, many of which would be very difficult with the use of other materials.

HISTORY OF WOOD IN LANDSCAPE ARCHITECTURE

Wood, in its most natural form, was probably the earliest building material, serving as the primary resource for shelters, weapons, and fuel for the early nomadic cultures. Of all the building materials, however, it is also one of the least permanent. Unless preserved through encapsulation by mud, lava, or sand and water, thus prohibiting the cycles of water penetration and drying, a majority of the examples of wood as it was used in antiquity have completely degraded. Most of the knowledge of early wood construction is based on fragments, drawings, and other written representations.

Wood as a feature of the built landscape can be found in nearly all cultures through history. Even in stone and masonry cultures with limited lumber resources, wood was used in the construction of pergolas, arbors, and other garden structures. Its many virtues include its relatively light weight, its ability to span long distances, flexibility, and workability. Its ease of extraction and use for house and boat building caused a depletion in many parts of the ancient world, and the once-wooded landscapes of the Mediterranean region have never recovered.

In ancient Rome timbers were largely reserved for shipbuilding and similar uses, but in hillside villa gardens, expansive wood beams reached across

Figure 1.1 View through the impluvium and across the peristyle at Villa Giulia Felix. Note the stone columns, wood beams, and rafters of the impluvium and the masonry columns and wood beams defining the peristyle on the far side. *Source:* J. Chatfield, *The Classic Italian Garden,* (New York: Rizzoli, 1991).

massive stone columns and formed trellised walkways lining canals, orchards, and ornamental gardens. Rafters, trellises, and doors were also typically constructed of wood.

The scale of the wood reconstruction of the peristyle and trellised walkways at Villa Guilia Felix illustrates how large openings between columns allow easy access inside and out (see Figure 1.1). The shade from the wood members above the walkway provides relief from the heat and a contrasting play of light with the bright sun-soaked open-air garden in the center. Unlike the Greeks, who considered their houses simply as a means of shelter, Romans considered the house and its enclosed gardens sacred (Chatfield, 1991, 12). Two further examples of these early Roman preserved houses and gardens can be seen at Villa dei Vettii and the villa of Loreius Tiburtinus in Pompeii.

The oldest known wood structure in the world still stands in Japan, a manifestation of the legacy of wood craftsmanship from its construction continuing through its restoration. The Horyu-ji Temple, with its spectacular five-storied tower building, Kondo, and elegant gate, is hard to specifically date (see Figure 1.2). The oldest buildings were lost in a fire in A.D. 670, and the new structures found on-site today have been continually rebuilt since the beginning of the eighth century; thus, the oldest buildings standing today, forming the central core, are approximately 1,300 years old. Japanese craftsmanship in wood is found at the highest level of mastery in court and monastery gardens from the Heian (784–1185) to the Edo (1615–1867) period. Elegance of line, pattern of order, and harmony in joining materials are illustrated in wood pavilions, bridges, fences, gates, and teahouses.

The early compounds, in which aristocratic mansions were surrounded with paradise gardens taken from descriptions of the idealistic Buddhist Pure Land, were part villa and part temple. Each wood member was scrutinized before it was cut or carved, with the master carpenter determining "what it wanted to be." Examples of wood and timber construction are found throughout the garden, in arching bridges spanning miniaturized rivers and in wood and bamboo fencing defining the interior spaces as separate from the exterior. In Shinden waterside pavilions the nearly transparent railings of the decks cantilevering over the ponds, along with the anchored stone foundations rising out of the water, are a remarkable integration of building and landscape.

One of the most famous Japanese garden structures, the Golden Pavilion in Kinkakuji (1397, Muromachi period) carries on the Shinden style. The

Figure 1.2 The oldest known wood structure in the world, the famous five-storied tower at Horyu-ji, has been rebuilt many times and reflects the enduring tradition of timber frame construction in Japanese building. *Source:* Mitchell Bring and Josse Wayembergh, *Japanese Gardens: Design and Meaning* (New York: McGraw-Hill, 1981).

main structure is linked to surrounding ancillary buildings through the elegant lines of the wooden bridgeways that appear to float above the lake.

A later approach, at the Katsura Imperial Villa (Edo period), incorporates unhewn structural posts to support the overhanging roof, uniting the human-built world with the surrounding pine tree forest.

The aesthetic and craft of the Japanese carpenter is found not just in the pavilions but also in the entry gates, such as at Shisendo (1641, Edo period), where wood and bamboo are brought together to create a rustic gateway to the garden. The same subtle harmony of scale and line is found in the small clear-span wooden bridges in the tea garden of Sambo-in (1598, Momoyama period). See Figure 1.3.

Intricacy of craftsmanship abounds in the Japanese garden in a variety of forms, ranging from the edge-defining kick rails at the Silver Pavilion in Ginkakuji (1482, Muromachi period) to the woven bamboo fences at Katsura Villa (Edo period).

A wholly different aesthetic is represented by the playful pattern of wood treilage used as the focal point in small, formal European gardens. Strips of hardwood are layered in an elaboration of trelliswork with references to architectural forms, like columns and pediments, and allusions to spatial depth with arched entryways (see Figure 1.4). Medieval European paintings and engravings depict wooden treilage used to embellish the walls of cloistered gardens and as latticework to define the walls of aviaries.

Seventeenth- and eighteenth-century constructions are shown in book illustrations as well. Flourishing at this time in France, Great Britain, and the

Figure 1.3   The wonderful horizontal-to-vertical relationships, simple joinery, and strong directional flow reveal the extraordinary "design skill and material appreciation" brought to this modest bridge. *Source:* From *Decorating Eden,* edited by Elizabeth Wilkinson and Marjorie Henderson © 1992. Published by Chronicle Books, San Francisco. Used with permission.

Figure 1.5 The wood fences, projecting from the building to create outdoor rooms, reiterate the architectural vocabulary found in the window lights in the greenhouse at Monticello. *Source:* University of Washington's CAUP slide collection.

Netherlands, treilage could quickly transform blank walls into architectural facades with illusory perspectives, a technique known as trompe l'oeil.

In the United States a rusticated example can be seen at Dunbarton Oaks in Washington, D.C., and a more elaborate, formal screen at the M. H. DeYoung Memorial Museum in San Francisco.

Notable examples from the mid-nineteenth century in Britain include the pergola at Bodnant, near Conwy, and the treilage wall/pergola at Dropmore, Buckinghamshire.

When used today, treilage is often fabricated in metal because of its longer life span. Recent innovations in material development, such as plastic lumber and expansion bolt anchoring systems, are yet to be explored for their potential in creating treilage. The use of forced perspective and architectonic forms may transform long stretches of blank walls into a blurring of building and open space.

As expansion moved westward and across the ocean, the building traditions of Europe began to appear across the landscape of the New World. One of the earliest American designers of the land, Thomas Jefferson, through the careful detailing of wooden fences and structures, was able to extend the architecture of a building into the landscape, creating beautiful outdoor rooms similar to those found in Europe. With the diagonal railings and fence cap details reflecting those of the building, he was able to unite architecture with the land, weaving the fence out into the fields and creating his agrarian landscape ideal at Monticello, his beloved home in Virginia (see Figure 1.5).

Jefferson, as one might expect, looked to Europe for ideas, but his attraction to the woodcraft of garden architecture expanded his interest in various other parts of the world. The objects he brought back to the states from his travels provided inspiration, as illustrated in the details found in his sketchbook for a wooden Chinese lattice bench. In fact, the many drawings of wooden garden structures planned for Monticello indicate Jefferson's fondness for wood as a landscape material in the late 1700s.

A century later, practitioners of landscape architecture not only pursued the design of residences but took on the design of the developing cities, the planning of cemeteries as botanical parks, and, as history has borne out, the creation of some of the greatest urban park systems in the world. The detailing of the many wooden park structures, entryways, and amenities incorporated a high level of woodcraft and design. The stylistic decisions were diverse and at times somewhat eccentric, but always in keeping with the principles of the picturesque, as pieces of bucolic countryside were being recreated in the growing urban centers of preindustrial America. Wood, in both its natural and its milled form, was commonly used for reconstruction of fencing, benches, bridges, and park pavilions. Many designers of the period found inspiration in John Ruskin's writings and in the natural world itself. In an attempt to reflect this celebration of and integration into the natural landscape, many landscape architects found that wood possessed the character and natural and/or manipulated form that best expressed these naturalist ideals. Examples include W. S. Cleveland's work on the bridge at Minnehaha Falls in the Minneapolis park system and Calvert Vaux's spectacular rusticated arbors and pavilions, now restored in Central Park, that became a vernacular style of the picturesque (see Figure 1.7).

The designer probably most influenced by Ruskin's writings and who felt impelled to link art (landscape architecture) and nature to morality and the love of God was the famous landscape designer Andrew Jackson Downing (see Figure 1.6). Ruskin advocated that craft not be lost in the industrial revolution and that expression through form and craftsmanship reflect the morals and character of humanity. In this pursuit, Downing explored and wrote about the craft of rustication, believing it most stylistically and environmentally appropriate to the rural landscape.

It possesses a good deal of character, is capable of considerable picturesque effect, is very easily and cheaply constructed of wood or stone, and is perhaps more entirely adapted to our hot summers and cold winters than any other equally simple mode of building. We hope to see the

Figure 1.6   A sketch of a rusticated gazebo, typical of the style practiced by Downing and others influenced by the writings of John Ruskin. Similar structures were found throughout the Hudson River Valley in the mid-nineteenth century. *Source:* From *Decorating Eden,* edited by Elizabeth Wilkinson and Marjorie Henderson © 1992. Published by Chronicle Books, San Francisco. Used with permission.

Bracketed style [a variation on rustication] becoming every day more common in the United Sates, and especially in our farm and country houses, when wood is the material employed in their construction (Tatum, 1991, 339).

Rustication is the use of wood in its most natural form. The limbed branches and trunks of a tree are used as building members with minimal tooling or cutting. The members are either jointed with mortise and tenons or lashed together. This technique was common in the mid- to late-nineteenth century and was used to build fences, seating, and even pavilions. As Downing noted, it conveys a natural or rural or wild character, and when used in an urban context was intended to reestablish that effect. Calvert Vaux and Fredrick Law Olmsted used it extensively in Central Park, and several pavilions and fencing have recently been restored (D. Robinson, D. Rosen, and A. Jaroslow, 1984). See Figure 1.7.

It was not only Jefferson who was influenced by distant cultures. The influence of the Impressionists—for example, Monet's bridge at Giverny as discernible in Cleveland's design for the wooden oriental bridge in Como Park, St. Paul—illustrates the cross-fertilization of cultures in the park elements of the day.

Figure 1.7 A rusticated pavilion restored in 1993 in New York's Central Park.

By the end of the nineteenth century and into the twentieth, a new stylistic influence could be found, particularly in the designs of the villas being created for the wealthy in New York and throughout New England. With the emphasis on Classical Revival architecture, such as found in the formal French and Italian gardens at the 1893 World's Colombian Exposition, many leaders in the arts and design communities, including Edith Wharton and Charles A. Platt, advocated the use of architectonic elements in gardens of the period. As an influential designer greatly affected by his travels in Italy, Charles A. Platt looked to the arbors, pergolas, and garden pavilions of Italy to extend the architecture of the villa out into the landscape. Whereas Jefferson had extended architectural elements into the garden through the use of fences, Platt viewed the design of the house and garden as an integrated whole, emphasizing the "total interrelationship of the architecture and landscape through an axial connection of major rooms with geometrically arranged garden units" (Tishler, 1989, 84).

The use of massive wooden arbors and pergolas to define these garden rooms can be seen at the surviving Falkner Farm, Brookline, Massachusetts, where the crescent-shaped pergola restates in a vertical manner the form of the reflecting pool below. Platt's predilection for Italian gardens and his desire to unify architecture and landscape through spatial relationships, and to define outdoor space with architectural elements, influenced a generation of landscape architects, many of whom looked elsewhere in Europe for inspiration (see Figures 1.8A and B).

A.

Figures 1.8 A and B   In his work at Faulkner Farm in Brookline, Massachusetts, Charles Platt reflected the growing interest in Italianate villa gardens. This pergola defines the edge of a flat lawn, and in so doing creates an open room, functioning as an extension of the villa out into the landscape. The masonry columns support curved box beams and cross members that function as a perimeter arcade.

B.

Figure 1.9   This pergola, designed by landscape architect Ellen Shipman, is composed of a gridded wood roof supported by masonry columns and creates a striking outdoor corridor. *Source:* William H. Tishler, *American Landscape Architecture,* copyright © 1989 John Wiley & Sons, Inc. Reprinted by permission of John Wiley & Sons, Inc.

Of these, Ellen Shipman employed wood for an overhead Italianate screen in the arbor at Wampus, a large estate in Mount Kisco, New York, and mastered an illusionary perspective through treilage in the wall treatment of the Dillman residence in Grosse Pointe, Michigan (see Figure 1.9).

Although many landscape architects looked to ideas emanating from France and Italy, others, including Beatrix Jones Farrand, turned to the work of English designers, such as Jekyll and Robinson, whose use of perennial borders and highly articulated architectural woodwork in their gardens inspired major projects in the United States. With its restraint of detail and celebration of craft, Farrand's arguably best work is seen at Dunbarton Oaks, where the delicate wooden gates in the herb garden provide access through the flanking boxwood hedge walls that define the gardens. The gates are small in size, but their white color provides a strong contrast to the dark greens of the boxwood.

As his work on the teahouse at Daisy Hill Farms reveals, A. D. Taylor brought the detailing of wood structures to a high level. His more than 40 editions of "Construction Notes," published in *Landscape Architecture* between 1922 and 1936, illustrate the level of quality and historical importance of the crafting of wood in the profession of landscape architecture. His column "Garden Details" featured the work of Taylor's firm, as well as that of guest authors, including Gilmore Clarke, Earle Draper, and Wheelright and Stevenson. The discussions focused on technical issues, as well as how wood structures might best be integrated into the landscape, and the virtues of vernacular styles of woodcraft and appropriate means of joinery were debated. This paragraph by Alfred Boerner, a landscape architect practicing in Milwaukee, from *Landscape Architecture* magazine, 1931, provides an example: "The simple type of beamed bridge was successfully constructed with a complete feeling of fitness in a natural setting some distance from a park drive and buildings. The design was reduced to the simplest form, satisfaction in effect being dependent entirely upon simple proportions and the choice and texture of materials used" (Boerner, 1931, 329). Such articles provided information on detailing wood constructions on a regular basis, including discussions of pergolas, fences, benches, and gates, among others (see Figures 1.10 and 1.11).

As the profession moved west, the use of wood in the garden achieved equally high levels in the Midwest, California, and the Northwest. In the Craftsman bungalow gardens of Greene and Greene and other practitioners, a style closer to Japanese prototypes reflects the art of joinery and highly crafted fasteners. Later, Garret Eckbo, Lawrence Halprin, and others referred to Japanese style in a modern reinterpretation known as the "California style," employing wood decks and louvered wood fencing that complemented the strong forms of the ground plane.

From this relatively small sampling it is clear that the craft of wood detailing and construction has played an important and evolving role in American and European landscape architecture. Yet it would be misleading to leave the reader with the impression that wood, as an innovative, expressive material, played a role only in residential gardens. The role of wood as a design element in the public and civic landscape is rich and important. Wood was used in parkway development in the early 1900s, when auto touring first became a recreational activity, and in the greenways along the river corridors that abutted the road alignments. Wood bridges and rusticated guardrails remain, in their simple vernacular, as symbols of the true "parkway." In the hands of skilled designers such as Gilmore D. Clarke (Bronx River Parkway) and Stanley W. Abbott (Blue Ridge Parkway), the level of wood detailing achieved in the fences and bridges in the "green" corridors along the roadways equals that found in residential projects. These wood structures helped to complete

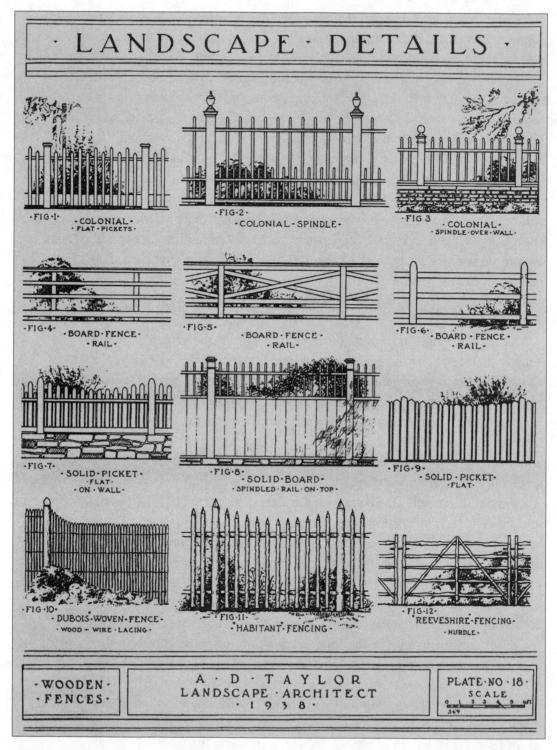

Figure 1.10   This page from A. D. Taylor's "Construction Notes" of wooden fences illustrates the variety of fence styles and degree of visual openness achieved through the baluster and picket spacings.

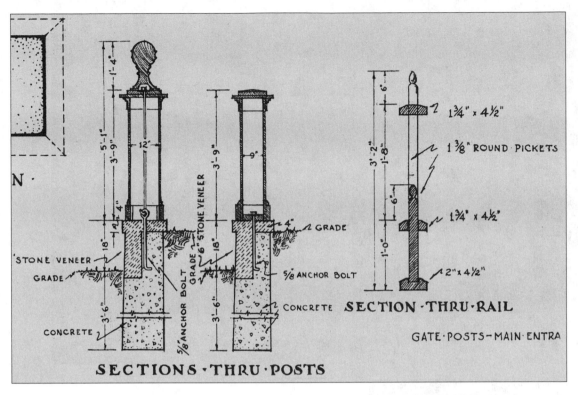

Figure 1.11   A page from A. D. Taylor's "Construction Notes" detail of hollow "thru" posts, railing, and finial.

the unique picturesque aesthetic that to this day is strikingly memorable along the Merritt, Taconic, Bronx River, and Blue Ridge Parkways. Clarke provided his details for a rusticated lighting pole for the Westchester County Parkway in a 1930 "Details of Construction" column in *Landscape Architecture* magazine. As the photos of the built lighting standard illustrate, the rough-hewn poles merge into the surrounding deciduous forest bordering the parkway. This vernacular also appears in the same magazine for a lapjointed rustic bumper rail for the Mount Vernon Memorial Highway, completed in 1932.

With a legacy of stewardship and a goal of integrating man and nature, the National Park Service (NPS) reflects a strong ethic based on a deep respect for the land. Through design, the NPS has developed its own vernacular, which can be found in the superb wood detailing in the visitors centers, bridges, and signage at Yellowstone and Yosemite. The same ethic is found in the naturalistic treatment of the bridges, boardwalks, and log shelters of the national forests, many designed by national forest and national parks land-

A.

B.

Figures 1.12 A and B   A. The day shelter at Moran State Park on San Juan Island, WA reflects the artful use of materials and massive scale typical of many of the wood constructions done under the Federal Works Administration. B. As exemplified in this picnic shelter at Moran State Park, a true integration of local stone and peeled logs defines the rustic vernacular that typifies the campground buildings built in the 1930s by the Civilian Conservation Corps (CCC), and in the 1940s under the Works Projects Administration (WPA). *Source:* Photographs by T. William Booth.

scape architects. The type of wood used and how it is split, bolted, or jointed, are conscious choices, based on the objective of complementing the wilderness experience with the use of natural materials.

This ethic of respect for nature, accompanied by a high level of craft and design innovation, reached its zenith during the 1930s, the period of the Civilian Conservation Corps (CCC). As the Depression's unemployed were brought from the cities and to the rural areas, they were taught, under the guidance of master craftsmen, the technical skills of joinery and the aesthetic of hand-hewing with indigenous materials. The result is a distinctive and powerful merging of the landscape and the built elements (see Figures 1.12 A and B).

Characteristic CCC work can be seen at Petit Jean State Park, Arkansas, where large wood beams rest on buttressed columns of rough-hewn stone and massive natural tree trunks are notched to receive smaller tree limbs as V bracing. Wood and stone work from this period is so distinct that these historic landscapes can be identified simply by sight and feel.

As this brief historical overview illustrates, wood has been used by landscape designers and architects as a material to define spaces (such as the fence at Monticello), to build highly ornamented or subtly integrated structures from which the landscape is viewed and contemplated (the Japanese teahouse), and to provide a simple means to cross over (bridges) or under (pergolas) a landscape space. Many designers, such as Calvert Vaux and Frederick Law Olmsted, A. D. Taylor, Thomas Church and Dan Kiley, have expressed a thoughtful understanding of wood as a unique building material and through their design celebrated the richness of the craft achievable in the hands of a master carpenter.

The following chapter describes the physical properties and characteristics of wood and the finishes, fasteners, and adhesives used. Chapter 3 presents the construction methodologies used to build several structures commonly designed in the practice of landscape architecture. Information on alternative materials and sustainable methods of wood product production can be found in the appendixes. A glossary of common terms and a list of relevant organizations and agencies follows the appendixes.

Figure 2.5   Glue-laminated members are often used in playground structures to span great distances and to create curved forms. This glulam bow arch supports a "wiggle bridge" that is hung from the steel chain.

2
MATERIALS AND PROPERTIES

WOOD COMPOSITION

The process of designing and building with wood is guided by an understanding of the basic characteristics of the material itself. The following sections provide an overview of the structural properties and characteristics of wood as a building material.

WOOD CHARACTER AND STRUCTURAL PROPERTIES

As a harvested living material, lumber is affected by a number of factors, including soil types, growth conditions, and natural calamities or periods of stress. Also influencing the character and properties of the final milled member are the location and orientation of the wood within the log, the presence of naturally occurring conditions, including knots (where branches were located), checks, splitting, sap deposits, and proximity of the wood to the bark layer.

A tree is composed of a series of long, hollow tubular structures or cells, aligned in a parallel direction along the trunk. The cells, composed of cellulose and hemicellulose, are attached with naturally occurring glues called lignin. During the growing season these cells, just below the bark layer, allow water to move up the tree, through small openings between cells in softwoods and through hollow vessels in hardwoods (McDonald, Falk, Williams, and Winandy, 1996, 1).

As new cells are formed during the growing season the wall of the previous year's growth thickens, creating the characteristic concentric "growth rings" that are visible in the cross-cut section of most trees. Most trees have two distinct annual growth periods, which produce differing densities of rings. The earlier growth formed during the spring, called earlywood or springwood, is less dense than that produced during the summer, the latewood or summerwood. The interface of the latewood of one season and the earlywood of the next produces the greatest density change. The character of the growth rings, including the properties and thickness of the cells, and the width of the rings depend on weather, the aspect of growth, and the age of the tree.

Because most cells are oriented parallel to the axis of the main trunk, the properties of the wood running perpendicular to the log are different from those of the wood running parallel to the log. Depending on the orientation of the cut in the milling process, three wood grain orientations are found: the *longitudinal direction,* the grain running parallel with the log, the *radial direction,* the grain running from the center of the log out to the bark, and the *tangential direction,* the grain running perpendicular to both the radial and longitudinal directions.

As the log is drawn through a saw, the orientation of the grain is established, depending on its relationship to the growth rings. Two contrasting conditions can occur (flat-grained, **c** in Figure 2.1), where the grain runs parallel to the longest end dimension, and vertical-grained (edge-grained, **a** in Figure 2.1), in which the grain is running parallel to the shortest dimension of the edge cut. These are the extremes, and in most sawn lumber the grain orientation is somewhere between flat and vertical.

Depending on its age, two types of wood occur in a log. Sapwood is the more recent growth, and as the tree creates new cells, the inner sapwood cells are transformed into heartwood, establishing the center of the log. Heartwood is usually distinguished from sapwood by its darker color. Although both provide structural strength to the living tree, the sapwood and inner bark serve as the circulatory system, transporting water and nutrients from the roots to the foliage. The heartwood serves as a structural inner core and does not transfer nutrients or water through the trunk, but does serve as a storage area for chemicals produced by the tree. These chemicals, called extractives, give the wood its natural color and, in a few species (red-

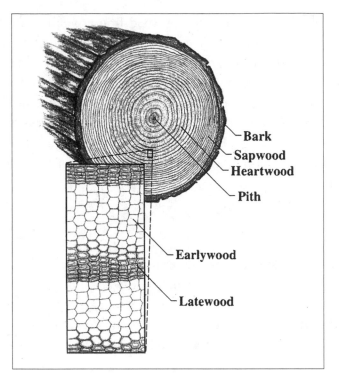
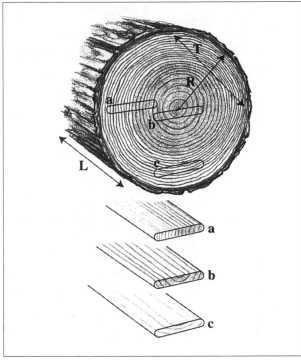

Figure 2.1   Cross section of log showing heartwood, sapwood, earlywood, latewood, and pith and the grain orientations determined by where the lumber is cut from the log. *(a)* Edge-grained (vertical grain). *(b)* Pith, a combination of edge and vertical grains. *(c)* Flat-grained. *Source:* K. A. McDonald, R. F. Falk, R. S. Williams, and J. E. Winandy, *Wood Decks, Materials, Construction, and Finishing* (Madison, Wisconsin: USDA, 1996).

wood, cedar, and locust), serve as natural preservatives against decay. Because heartwood is composed of essentially dead cells that no longer function as a circulatory system and, as compared with sapwood, is resistant to water migration, it is prized for use in exterior wood construction. The end grain part of board lumber is the most vulnerable, inasmuch as water can easily migrate through the cell structure, particularly when the board is cut from the sapwood. When lumber is used in exterior applications, all end grain that is exposed to moisture should be treated with a preservative.

Knots are identified as circular discolorations with a density differing from that of the surrounding wood. Knots are the result of branches or limbs growing from the main trunk. When a branch is lost, part of it may be encased in the trunk as the tree continues to grow. In trees of a large girth the encased portion is typically in the center heartwood and the outer wood is often free of knots. On younger trees the branches extend through the sapwood, producing an abundance of knots in the wood from a young, fast-growth tree. If a knot has resulted from a living branch, it is referred to as a tight knot and is usually structurally secure. If a knot has resulted from a dead branch, it may not be connected to the surrounding wood and may loosen and fall out of the board, leaving a hole. The structural performance of a wood member is hindered by loose knots occurring at points of stress or where fasteners are attached. In the grading of lumber, knots are evaluated for their size, frequency, location, form, and type (tight or loose) to assess the quality and value of the wood.

MOISTURE CONTENT

Once cut, wood begins to dry out, losing water from its cells by evaporation. If the discharge of moisture is left uncontrolled, the wood may dry too quickly, causing either splitting around the end grain or warpage within the board. A number of distortions to a board's shape can occur after milling and grading, and the following common conditions can be visually identified (see Figure 2.2).

Cupping: Cupping occurs when the two flat faces of a board dry at different rates. Cupping in 1 × 4s or 2 × 6s may be seen as the profile of the board's end grain curves in from the sides, creating a cupped form on the faces. In a decking situation, if the concave side is oriented up, it will collect water, increasing the potential for decay, and with the repeated pressure of foot traffic the board will eventually crack. The prevalence of cupping is higher in boards with a flat grain than in those with a vertical grain. The degree of cupping depends on density, moisture content during milling, control of the drying process, thickness, width, and grain orientation. Boards tend to cup away from the bark side of the wood, and when used in decking,

Figure 2.2   Distortions commonly found in board lumber:
A. Cupping.
B. Bowing
C. Crooking
D. Twisting
Source: Illustration by Jody Estes.

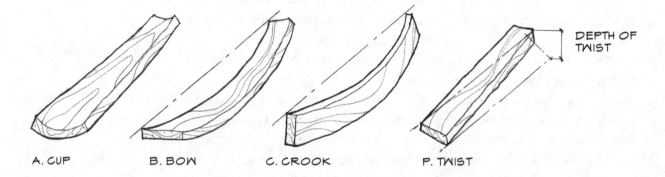

A. CUP   B. BOW   C. CROOK   D. TWIST

the term "bark side up" refers to the laying of the decking boards with the growth rings facing down and the convex side up, thus preventing the board from entrapping water. Live loads on a deck tend to flatten the boards and reduce the mounding that can occur in the bark-side-up orientation.

Bowing, Crooking, Twisting: These distortions occur along the length of a board. Bowing may be seen, siting the board down its narrow edge as a single curving of its face plane. Crooking is observed by looking down the face plane to find the board curving on itself at the edge dimension. Twisting is a combination of curves in different directions. Minor distortions of these types can often be reversed as the boards are tied into a structure. All major structural members have to be true and free of distortions. Lumber deliveries must be inspected at the job site, and unsuitable material should be rejected.

These distortions to lumber most frequently occur during an accelerated and uneven drying process. Wood is best seasoned either by the air-drying (AD) or the kiln-drying (KD) process. In each process the wood is cured so that the moisture is released in a controlled manner, reducing potential for distortion. In both methods the wood is stacked with spacers placed between the boards, allowing air and heat to flow between and around the wood members. The spacers should be aligned vertically, transferring the weight evenly throughout the spacers. If this is not done, or the wood is not stacked with the appropriate weight to resist warpage, distortions can occur. Drying time varies according to species, lumber thickness, and the moisture content of the wood and the air. To dry a ½ in. thick piece of lumber, at least two months of dry summer weather is needed. With the mechanical circulation of air, this time can be reduced to one month. (McDonald et al., 1996, 24). With kiln drying, time is further reduced; however, if the kiln temperature is set too high and the process accelerated, severe warping can occur. Wood is sold with moisture content ranging from less than 15% to more than 19%. A 2 × 4 with a moisture content of less than 15% will be noticeably lighter, with an average weight 33% less than its cut "green" counterpart.

The optimum moisture content of lumber for stability in a structure is 12%. Even after it is dried, wood is still susceptible to variations in size as a result of moisture absorption. As a general rule, wood expands as it gains and shrinks as it loses moisture. The change occurs as the member goes from its dry state to its fiber saturation point, the point at which the wood fibers can take on no more water, or as the reverse occurs. The degree of change depends on the amount of moisture absorbed, the species of wood, and the cut of the grain. It is interesting to note that in tests conducted by the USDA Forest Products

RELATED SPECIFICATIONS
01300—Submittals
01400—Quality Control

Laboratory, the change in longitudinal dimension is essentially zero as compared with the tangential and radial directions. The results show that shrinkage is considerably less in the radial direction than in the tangential, which is one of the reasons that vertical wood is preferred over other grain orientations.

SIZING AND SURFACING

Lumber comes in standardized thicknesses, widths, and lengths, but it can be custom milled to meet any nonstandardized dimensions. The "nominal dimension" is the actual thickness and width of the wood following its initial cut from the log at the sawmill. The terms *surfaced* or *dressed* refer to the wood members after they have been finish planed. The nominal member is run through a planing machine, a series of blades attached to a cylindrical drum, that removes ¼ in. of surface material per side. The resulting dimensions, if surfaced on four sides, will be ½ in. less in both the edge (thickness) and the face (width) dimensions than those of a nominally dimensioned board of the same size. A designation of S4S means surfaced on four sides; a designation of S2S, two sides. It is important to note that the term *two-by-four* refers to a surfaced member, which is smaller in cross-sectional area than a 2 in. by 4 in. piece of rough lumber. Its actual measurements when dry and surfaced on four sides will be 1½ in. × 3½ in. It is possible to get rough, "unsurfaced" nominally dimensioned lumber, but it is not graded and does not have structural design values. Structural lumber is commonly available in the softwood species, including "dimensional lumber," members that are nominally 2 to 4 in. thick, and "timbers," lumber greater than 5 in. in thickness. The thinnest standardized dressed thickness for lumber is ½ in., increasing in thickness to ¾, ⁵⁄₄, 1½, and 3½ in. and more. If the size of a required member exceeds the limits of a log, several members can be glue laminated together to create the desired dimensions.

RELATED SPECIFICATIONS
01300—Submittals
01400—Quality Control

LUMBER GRADING

Because lumber characteristics vary according to species, size of members, and intended use, a grading system has been established to make various designations reasonably uniform throughout the country. The first grading efforts were initiated in the 1880s in the Great Lakes region. Mill operators, builders, architects, and officials from the U.S. Department of Commerce, in a collaborative effort, established the first nationwide grading rules in the 1920s. Lumber grading takes place at the sawmills and in the United States is supervised by one of ten agencies accredited by the American Lumber Standard Committee (ALSC), which is also responsible for writing the standards used for lumber milling and grading.

All dressed softwood lumber, treated or untreated, and all glulams receive a lumber grade stamp. The stamp, applied to the wood members by an approved grading or inspection agency, is mandatory, required by building codes throughout the country for all lumber used for structural purposes. The designation allows designers, builders, and inspectors to specify and inspect wood members as appropriate to a particular project. The lumber grade mark uses standardized symbols to list five pieces of information: grade designation (quality), species identification, the maximum moisture content at the time of surfacing, the grading agency responsible for the inspection, and the mill identification. These symbols are used nationwide and are required to be visible for confirmation at the job site (see Figure 2.3).

Grading, conducted at the mill by certified graders, is a visual inspection to assess strength and/or appearance. Graders look for frequency, size, quality, and location of knots, cross grain, and any natural decay, splits, wanes, or milling flaws.

The first piece of information, and in most stamps the largest symbol shown, is the lumber grade. Lumber grades are divided into four performance standards: light framing, structural light framing, structural joists and planks, and those designated for use as studs, vertical members used in load-bearing walls. These can be further broken down into grade names, which are designations based on quality variation. For example, the light framing category includes construction, standard, and utility grades, with construction being the highest and utility the lowest. These divisions are predominately based on appearance, inasmuch as all qualify for the use of light framing. The quality of wood is designated by use in the grade stamp and is labeled by number (such as #2), by name (stud), or by abbreviation (STAND for standard).

Several species, such as redwood and cedar, are available in appearance as well as structural grades. These qualities of presentation are of greater value than structural qualities in selecting siding, flooring, and trim. Decking lumber, for example, is available only in appearance grades, and although boards selected by appearance grade are not usually designated for design values, better appearance generally means greater strength. The factors inspected for appearance grade include grain orientation, presence of heart- or sapwoods,

Interpreting Grade Marks

Most grade stamps, except those for rough lumber or heavy timbers, contain 5 basic elements:

a. **Certification trademark.** Certifies Association quality supervision. ® is a registered trademark.

b. **Mill identification.** Firm name, brand or assigned mill number.

c. **Grade designation.** Grade name, number or abbreviation.

d. **Species identification.** Indicates species by individual species or species combination. Species identification marks for groups to which design values are assigned are:

SPF^s · WEST WOODS · WEST CDR

e. **Condition of seasoning.** Indicates condition of seasoning at time of surfacing:

MC-15 — 15% maximum
KD-15   moisture content

S-DRY — 19% maximum
KD   moisture content

S-GRN — over 19% moisture content (unseasoned)

Inspection Certificate

When an inspection certificate issued by an **agency** is required on a shipment of lumber and specific grade marks are not used, the stock is identified by an imprint of the Association mark and the number of the shipping mill or inspector.

Grade Stamp Facsimiles

Agencies use a set of marks, similar to the randomly selected examples shown on the next page, to identify lumber graded under its supervision.

Species Combinations

The species groupings for dimension lumber products are shown in the first box and explained in the second box on the next page. When alternative species combinations, as shown in the third box on the next page, are used for structural applications, design values are controlled by the species with the lowest strength value within the combination.

Figure 2.3   A certified grade stamp. Used to designate the grade of lumber, moisture content, species, mill and grading agency. *Source:* © Western Wood Products Association, Portland, Oregon. ® 1997 WWPA. All symbols and text used by permission of the WWPA.

quantity, size, and quality of knots, and other natural or manufacturing flaws. The designations include "tight knot" and "clear."

The second piece of information included in the grade stamp is the species of tree from which the wood was milled, and this is indicated by name (e.g., redwood), abbreviation (D Fir for Douglas fir) or symbol (PP for ponderosa pine). Some symbols designate a combination of species that have similar mechanical properties, such as SPF for spruce-pine-fir.

Species Identification

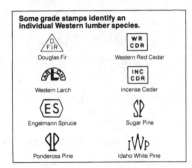

Some grade stamps identify an individual Western lumber species.

Douglas Fir	Western Red Cedar
Western Larch	Incense Cedar
Engelmann Spruce	Sugar Pine
Ponderosa Pine	Idaho White Pine

A number of Western lumber species have similar performance properties and are marketed with a common species designation. These species groupings are used for lumber to which design values are assigned.

DOUG. FIR-L — Douglas Fir and Larch	D FIR S — Douglas Fir South*
HEM FIR — California Red Fir, Grand Fir, Noble Fir, Pacific Silver Fir, White Fir and Western Hemlock	SPF S — Engelmann and Sitka Spruce, Lodgepole Pine (and Eastern firs and spruces)
WEST WOODS — Alpine Fir, Ponderosa Pine, Sugar Pine, Idaho White Pine and Mountain Hemlock, plus any of the species in the other groupings except Western Cedars	WEST CDR — Incense, Western Red Port Orford and Alaska Cedar

*Lumber manufactured from Douglas Fir grown in Arizona, Colorado, Nevada, New Mexico and Utah.

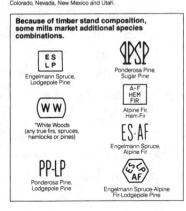

Because of timber stand composition, some mills market additional species combinations.

ES LP — Engelmann Spruce, Lodgepole Pine	PSP — Ponderosa Pine, Sugar Pine
WW — *White Woods (any true firs, spruces, hemlocks or pines)	A-F HEM FIR — Alpine Fir, Hem-Fir
PP-LP — Ponderosa Pine, Lodgepole Pine	ES-AF — Engelmann Spruce, Alpine Fir / ES LP AF — Engelmann Spruce-Alpine Fir-Lodgepole Pine

Facsimiles of Typical Grade Stamps

Dimension Grades

Glued Products

Finish Grade — Graded Under WCLIB Rules

Cedar Grades

12 CLEAR MC 15 — VG HEART — WR CDR

12 A MC 15 — WEST CDR

Commons

12 4 COM — S-DRY — ES

12 STERLING — S-DRY — IWP

Machine Stress-Rated Products

MACHINE RATED — 12 — S-DRY — D FIR — 1650 Fb 1.5E

MACHINE RATED — 12 — S-DRY — D FIR — 1650Fb 1020Ft 1.5E

Finish & Select Grades

12 C & BTR SEL — MC 15

12 PRIME — MC 15 — D FIR

12 D SEL — MC 15 — SP

Decking

12 SEL DECK — MC 15 — INC CDR

12 PATIO 1 — S-DRY

Moisture content, the third piece of information provided, is important in evaluating how much shrinkage, and potentially distortion, can be expected from a board. The amount of moisture is shown as either an abbreviation or as a number. The symbol S-GRN (surfaced green) indicates that the board was milled with a moisture content of more than 19% and that it was cut slightly oversized so that when dried to a 19% moisture content, it will have the same dimensions as S-DRY (surfaced dry) planed at 19% or less.

The fourth piece of information, the certification symbol, identifies the agency (Northeastern Lumber Manufacturers Association [NELMA], for example) that supervised the grading. The fifth, the mill symbol, designated by name or number (e.g., 38), identifies the mill where the lumber was cut.

Solid lumber used for engineered components and glulams are graded mechanically and designated as MSR (machine stress rated). The members are inspected both mechanically and visually. The stamps indicate the species, assign one of four grades (construction, standard, utility, and stud), and give two stress test measurements. The fiber stress bending (Fb) figure is a measure of tensile and compressive forces, and the modulus of elasticity (E) figure indicates how much deflection will occur under certain loads (see Figure 2.4).

GLUE-LAMINATED LUMBER

With the development of wet-use adhesives—urea and resorcinal—in combination with pressure-treated wood lumber, structural glue-laminated members designed for exterior use have become practical and cost-efficient. Laminated beams comprise two or more boards, customarily 1½ in. up to 2 in. thick, which are glued and face bonded along their widest sides and put under pressure to adhere. Glulams are fabricated from conventional lengths of lumber, with the wood grain running parallel to the length of the member. The ends can be structurally finger-jointed together to create long or curved structural members.

The standardized widths range from 3⅛ in. to 6¾ in. The depths range from 6 to 36 in., although virtually any depth is available by custom order. Lengths are limited only by the capacity of the shop, the glue bed, and the conveyance vehicle. Special beam lay-ups (placment and orientation of the individual wood members) are possible, in which the strongest laminations are placed in the zones of the highest forces of tension or compression.

For exterior applications, members can be fabricated out of naturally resistant heartwoods of redwood or red or Alaskan cedar, but because of cost or an environmental ethic, pressure-treated coastal Douglas fir, hem-fir, western hemlock, and southern pine are more frequently used. For these woods,

Figure 2.4   Yard lumber sizes and grading. *Source:* Adapted from Caleb Hornbostel, *Construction Materials,* copyright © John Wiley & Sons, Inc. New York, 1978. Reprinted by permission of John Wiley & Sons, Inc.

Grade Categories

Grade category	Maximum edge knot (in.)*	Wane	Warp (in.)[†]	
			Crook	Twist
Structural Light Framing 2 X 4 High Strength Design Values				
Select Structural	3/4	1/4 thickness	1/2	9/16
		1/4 width		
No. 1	1	1/4 thickness	1/2	9/16
		1/4 width		
No. 2	1 1/4	1/3 thickness	11/16	3/4
		1/3 width		
No. 3	1 3/4	1/2 thickness	1	1 1/8
		1/2 width		
Light Framing 2 X 4 Basic Framing Lumber				
Construction	1 1/2	1/4 thickness	1/2	9/16
		1/4 width		
Standard	2	1/3 thickness	11/16	3/4
		1/3 width		
Utility	2 1/2	1/2 thickness	1	1 1/8
		1/2 width		
Stud 2 X 4 Optional Grade for Vertical Use				
Stud	1 3/4	1/3 thickness	3/8	7/16
		1/2 width		
Structural Joists and Planks 4 X 12				
Select Structural	1	1/4 thickness	1/2	
		1/4 width		
No. 1	3	1/4 thickness	1/2	
		1/4 width		
No. 2	3 3/4	1/3 thickness	Light	
		1/3 width		
No. 3	5 1/2	1/2 thickness	Medium	
		1/2 width		

Adapted from U.S.D.A. Forest Services Labratory, 1996 and Western Lumber Grading Rules, 1998.

*Larger sizes would have proportionally larger permissible knots.

†Assuming a 12-foot length, various sizes would have progressively higher or lower limits.

Stud grade assumes a 10-foot length.

with the exception of southern pine, incising is recommended in pressure treating, and appearance should be considered in designing with pressure-treated glulams (see Figure 2.5, p. 20).

Preservatives vary in how they interfere with adhesion in the laminating process, depending on the type selected. Using preservatives such as creosote, creosote solutions, creosote petroleum, or pentachlorophenol in heavy petroleum oils to treat wood prior to lamination is not recommended. Waterborne preservatives can be used for treatment of wood members before lamination. A number of treatments are restricted, depending on the intended use. The Environmental Protection Agency (EPA) regulations should be consulted. For more information on preservatives, see "Wood Preservative Treatments" on pages 41–43.

If a member is particularly long or a curve is deep, the supplier should be contacted prior to design to confirm that the member specified can fit into the cylindrical treatment tank.

Like other preservative-treated lumber, treated glulams should not be cut, bored, or damaged in transit to or on the job site after being treated. When this is unavoidable, all cuts, borings, or damages that penetrate the surface layer should be field treated and fumigants should be placed in pre-bored holes to arrest internal decay.

RELATED SPECIFICATIONS
06100 — Rough Carpentry
06130 — Heavy Timber
Construction
06170 — Prefabricated
Structural Wood

FINISHES AND COATINGS

Many of the most common problems of mildew, decay, checking, and splitting found in wood used in exterior construction can be minimized through proper finishing and maintenance. The range and severity of climatic conditions, including exposure to direct sun and ultraviolet (UV) rays, rain, snow, and wind, increase the importance of proper protection. Horizontal decking, for example, is particularly prone to slippage caused by growth of molds, and vertical members are vulnerable to moisture infiltration by wicking at their concrete footings and infiltration at exposed, unprotected end grains. Exterior wood can benefit in longevity and performance from regular applications of a suitable finish.

Wood finishing products can be divided into two types: penetrating products that are absorbed through the surface into the cells of the wood, and film-forming finishes that, in the process of curing, form a skin that seals the material beneath. Both are designed to protect the wood from ultraviolet degradation and weathering and are used to enhance the surface appearance by evening or preserving the natural color variation or by creating a new color altogether. Those considered penetrating finishes include semitransparent stains, water repellents, repellent preservatives, and chemical treatments.

The film-forming materials include paints, varnishes, solid color stains, lacquers, and texture coatings. In general terms, these finishes are composed of three elements. The pigment provides color and repels ultraviolet light, protecting the surface beneath. The binder functions to hold the various elements—pigments, preservative chemicals, and retardants or accellerants—together, provides an adhesion to the substrate, and creates the film. The carrier keeps the pigments and binders in liquid form. The determining factor for a film-forming or penetrating type of finish is largely the formulation of the binder.

FILM-FORMING FINISHES

The film-forming group of finishes constitutes a wide variety of oil- and water-based finishes that range from solid color stains and paints to semi-transparent stains and transparent varnishes and lacquers.

Paints

The most common wood finishing paints can be grouped in two categories: oil-based and alkyd paint products and acrylic latex products. The oil and alkyd paints are composed of inorganic pigments suspended in an oil or resin vehicle, which binds the pigments and bonding agent to the wood surface. Petroleum-based or turpentine-based solvents are used for thinning and cleaning. The latex-based paints are also composed of suspensions of inorganic pigments, with latex resins as the binding vehicle. Acrylic latex paints can be thinned and cleaned with water. For many years oil-based paints were recommended for exterior use; however, today the trend seems to be reversing, as acrylic latex coatings are very durable, maintain flexibility to respond as wood expands and contracts, and often have a longevity equal to that of a good oil-based paint. The latex paints are also porous and can breathe while still shedding water, which may contribute to their durability.

Paints, ubiquitously used on the siding of houses, provide good protection from weathering to the wood beneath the coating, including the retardation of moisture penetration, the elimination of UV degradation, and the prevention of discoloring extractives on the surface. Paints, among all the finishes, offer the widest range of colors, shades, and textures, but should not be considered preservatives. The film that forms on the surface helps to prevent water penetration but does not prevent fungal growth. Paints have limited application on highly traveled surfaces such as decks and play structures inasmuch as the film surface increases the potential for slippage. There are specially formulated paints that use additives (e.g., walnut shells) to create coarse textures and provide greater resistance to slippage. The use of paints on decking and other horizontal surfaces is also limited because standing surface water can penetrate the film, causing paint to uplift and eventually peel away from the wood. If a paint is used on a deck or porch, the wood should be treated with a paintable water repellent (WRP) and a high-quality deck enamel, specially designed to resist abrasion and wear, should be applied. For horizontal wearing surfaces a WRP or semitransparent penetrating stain may be a better choice.

A number of variables influence the durability of paint finishes, including the species and character of the wood, type of paint, ambient temperature during and after application, moisture content of the wood, and type of undercoating (primers) used. There are some wood species that perform better with certain finishes than others. Because all woods shrink and swell, those that deform least work best with film finishes, as less movement of the wood results in less stress on a film finish and, thus, less potential for cracking. The extent of swelling is related to the density of the wood. Woods with low densities (e.g., western red cedar and redwood) are better for paint finishes than the denser species. The softwoods, such as pine and fir, providing they are planed and do not contain many knots, perform well. For the best paint performance, painting should be done on a stable and fairly smooth surface. To extend the service life of the paint, all exposed end grains, the most vulnerable points of water infiltration, and, if possible, all exterior wood surfaces should be treated with a paintable water repellent or water repellent preservative prior to the paint application.

In using woods with knots or species with color extractives that are prone to bleeding (cedar and redwood), a stain-blocking primer should be used to seal the wood and prevent pitch or color from bleeding up through the paint coat. These primers, identified as "stain killers" or "stain sealers," are generally shellac-based binders with a white pigmentation added. The primer is applied to the wood surface of extractive species, or spot applied on knots if the wood is a species not prone to color bleeding, before paint is applied.

Primers are undercoatings that seal the wood surface and provide a bond coat for either oil or latex finish applications. The wood should be dry before the primer, uniform in thickness, is applied. Once dry, the finish coats can be applied over the prime coat with brushes, rollers, or in a spray application. Two finish coats should be applied. To avoid separation, the first coat should be applied within two weeks of the prime coat and the second finish coat within two weeks of the first; otherwise a film can form, inhibiting paint adhesion.

Oil-based paints can be applied at temperatures above 40°F, and latex paints require temperatures above 50°F for a duration of at least 24 hours after application.

Oil and Latex Solid Color Stains

Oil and latex solid color stains, also called opaque stains, are both penetrating and film forming. Many solid color stains contain preservatives and water repellents, usually paraffin wax dissolved in solvents. The preservative and solvents penetrate the wood surface, leaving the pigmentation and binder on the surface, which form a film. These products are not successful on horizontal surfaces used for traffic as the pigments are not stable.

Latex Semitransparent Stains

Latex semitransparent stains, despite their name, do not penetrate the wood surface but, instead, leave a thin film coating on the surface. The stains are emulsions of polymers (acrylics or acrylic blends) and provide protection for most wood surfaces. They are not, however, recommended for coating decking boards.

Varnishes and Lacquers

Varnishes and lacquers are clear and lack natural pigmentation to protect wood; thus, UV light penetrates the finish, degrading the wood below. Most of these finishes have extremely limited life spans, typically a year in exterior conditions. The use of colorless UV inhibitors has been moderately successful, but the weatherproofing qualities of even the synthetic clear polymers are limited, as the UV light degrades the underlying wood surfaces, undermining the adhesion. If varnishes are to be used on exterior structures, the choice of location may present the greatest opportunity for durability. If possible, site the structure in an area that receives little or no direct sunlight, because exposure to UV rays causes the greatest damage.

Pigments can be added to both varnishes and lacquers to reveal the color and grain of the surface or to provide a surface coloring. If varnishes or lacquers are to be used on previously finished wood, any remaining finish must be removed before refinishing is attempted.

RELATED SPECIFICATIONS
09900—Painting

PENETRATING FINISHES

Penetrating finishes are particularly advantageous for use on wood. These finishes are not prone to peeling, and they allow the wood to breathe. By repelling water and moisture infiltration, penetrating finishes extend the life of the wood. Such a finish can be used as an undercoating for film finishes or simply applied as a finish in itself.

Both unpigmented water repellents and water-repellent preservatives, which are clear finishes, contain a water repellent, often a wax with a binder. Ten to 20% of the solution is the binding agent, typically a tung or linseed oil that provides penetration and, when dry, partially seals the surface. The binder also serves as an adhesive, binding mildewcides and water repellents to the wood. The quantity of repellent varies, depending on the mix, and those finishes with a low concentration (1%) can be used as undercoatings and those with higher concentrations (3% or more) as final finishes. The primary difference between water repellents and water-repellent preservatives (WRPs) is that a WRP contains a mildewcide, a chemical additive that prevents the buildup of mildews and molds.

Both of these finishes extend the life of the wood by repelling water, thereby reducing the amount of moisture absorption, decreasing dimensional changes, and preventing warpage, splitting, and twisting.

Most waterborne treatments available do not contain mildewcides, and a WRP should be added to these to prevent fungal degradation. A WRP provides some aboveground resistance for parts of a wood member that did not have preservative treatment in production, such as the heartwood, or for areas that have been crosscut, ripped, or bored after the preservative treatment was applied.

There are some preservatives that contain nondrying oils as solvents; these penetrate the wood surface to a greater depth but take much longer for complete absorption. These finishes provide good results for moisture resistance, but because the drying may take several days, depending on the species and moisture content of the wood, the use and workability of the wood will be restricted.

Semitransparent Stains. When a WRP solution or a similar transparent finish is combined with a pigment, the resulting finish is classified as a semitransparent stain. The addition of the pigmentation inhibits UV penetration, increasing the life of the wood. Because semitransparent stains reveal the wood grain through a transparent glaze of color, they offer a different aesthetic from that produced by opaque stains. These stains, containing a solvent-borne oil-based binder, completely penetrate the wood, leaving no film on the surface. This results in a finish that is impervious to peeling and blistering, reducing the amount of maintenance required. Solvent-based stains can be reapplied on wood that has been previously treated with solvent-based penetrating stains. A latex-based stain forms a film layer and will not perform like a true semitransparent stain.

Semitransparent stains are applicable on both smooth and rough wood surfaces, but perform best on rough-sawn, weathered, or coarse-textured wood surfaces—surfaces on which paint functions poorly.

The traditional semitransparent stain is designed for use on siding, rails, fences, gates, and so forth. A second and more recent development is a semitransparent stain designed with improved abrasion resistance for use on decks and other walking surfaces. The quality of the stain is determined by the amount and type of pigmentation, resins, preservatives, and water repellent, which ultimately determine its durability.

If the wood has been previously treated with a WRP material at the factory, semitransparent stains may not be fully absorbed into the wood. The wood should be left to air dry until it is fully absorbent before a semitransparent stain is applied.

RELATED SPECIFICATIONS
06300 — Wood Treatment
09900 — Painting

Mildewcides. Mildewcides can be added to film-forming and penetrating finishes before application or can be formulated into paints, semitransparent and transparent stains, and WRPs at the manufacturing plant. Mildewcides differ from the treatments applied at the pressure treating plants, such as chromated copper arsenate (CCA) or ammoniacal copper zinc arsenate (ACZA), which are useful only in preventing fungal decay. A number of mildewcides are used in WRPs, including 3-Iodo-2-propynyl butyl carbamate (polyphase), thiocyanomethylthio benzothiazole (TCMTB), and zinc naphthanate, all of which are available in solvent or waterborne formulations. Other treatments, including copper naphthanate, are very effective in treating the ends of treated members that have been cut and, with mildewcides added, are among the few wood treatments used for below-grade decay resistance. Copper naphthanate and other copper-based treatments will, through the oxidation process, turn a wood surface various shades of green and may not be aesthetically appropriate in certain applications.

Since 1980 growing public concern over the use of toxic preservative chemicals has caused the restriction of some solvent-based mildewcides, and as a result a number of waterborne formulations have been introduced (see "Wood Preservative Treatments," pages 41–43). Some manufacturers are producing low volatile organic compound (VOC) formulations in response to concerns about ozone depletion. Most states have legislation in place limiting the VOC levels in finishes, and manufacturers are now producing low VOC water repellents and WRPs for public use. See "Nontoxic and Low VOC Finishes," pages 181–183.

CONSIDERATIONS FOR CHOOSING FINISHES

A number of factors can affect the performance of finishes, including the type of finish selected, moisture content, natural weathering, and the quality and species of the wood on which the finish is applied.

All species of wood are susceptible to degradation from UV saturation and the natural effects of weathering. Penetrating stains break down, but at a slower rate than unfinished wood, and pigments increase UV resistance; however, once degradation of the finish begins, the pigment particles debond and the protection is reduced. To prevent debonding, additional stain applications may be required.

Film-forming finishes (paints) offer two advantages. The film coating effectively blocks UV saturation and is a sacrificial coating, protecting the wood surface from abrasion. The most damaging elements to the wood and to film coatings are moisture penetration and the UV portion of light exposure, which over time will break down a film coating.

Film finishes, providing protection against surface erosion, allow visual inspection to determine when the primer is visible and an additional coat should be applied. Many successive coats may be applied if the surface contact to the wood has not been disturbed, which can extend the life of the material. If water does penetrate through the film, decay below the film can be extensive and should be addressed immediately with removal of the loose layer.

Moisture is the most common factor in wood decay, particularly when it is trapped beneath a film finish. If moisture saturates the wood, causing swelling, the film-forming finishes will fracture, allowing water to seep into the wood finish interface, breaking the bond, and over time resulting in a peeling away of the film from the wood surface. Where two wood members connect, the joints, when exposed to the elements, are most vulnerable to water infiltration and decay. The rail to post, beam to post, and balustrade to rail interfaces are particularly vulnerable. When water collects at these points, any fracturing of the finish allows water to penetrate beneath the coating and into the wood. Any movement within the structure or impact to these joints can cause fractures in the finish coating, leading to water infiltration. Because the contact points in many joints are end grain to surface wood, or end grain to end grain, such as in a railing cap or post base, the water rapidly seeps into the end grain, migrating through the wood member and causing decay within it (see Figure 2.6). Often, the remaining film entraps water and wood degradation continues unnoticed until the member is structurally compromised (see Figure 2.7).

As mentioned previously, because wood may not be 100% dry material, it is important that when a finish is applied, the moisture content of the material be as close as possible to the moisture content in its place of installation so as to achieve the greatest service from the finish. The desired moisture content in the United States is about 12%, although the content of treated wood is often higher and storage in lumberyards will affect different bundles. This situation is less critical when a penetrating finish is to be used, because drying may still continue after the finish is applied, a process not possible in film finishes. A moisture content of less than 20% is recommended before applying any finishing. At this percentage the wood surface will feel dry to the touch, but for greater accuracy a moisture sensor can be employed. It should be noted that even if the outer surface feels dry, the interior may have a moisture content well above 20% and the wood should be air-dried or left in the sunlight until the moisture content is reduced. This moisture reduction treatment requires careful monitoring, because wood exposed to drying elements for long periods will suffer slight surface weathering effects, which can hinder the ability of the finishes to bond to the wood.

The species of wood chosen will affect the performance of the finish. Several factors are at play, including density, percentage of latewood, decay

Figure 2.6   Lead flashing, easily molded, can be formed to fit around and into concave/convex forms. In this example the painted flashing is formed around the column base and into the grooves to prevent water infiltration.

Figure 2.7   Any movement in the framing, box post, or moldings can cause paint fractures, leading to moisture infiltration, decay, and, unless corrected, complete replacement. Patched wood repairs to a box post indicate the extent of the damage. Note the diagonal mitered joint used to connect the old to the new wood.

resistance, dimensional stability, and weathering. These factors affect a film finish more than a penetrating finish, although periodic applications of a penetrating product will be required to minimize surface degradation.

Although lower-density woods (e.g., cedar and redwood) have high absorption rates and will accept film and penetrating finishes well, they tend to color bleed as the natural tannins rise to the surface and penetrate the finish, causing surface discoloring. These particular species have good dimensional stability, which is important to ensure a lasting film-forming finish. The higher-density woods, such as southern pine, with wide bands of latewood are less absorbent and stable, thus increasing the maintenance requirements for certain finishes.

The quality of the wood selected and the number and size of knots will affect the quality of film-forming finishes. The higher amounts of resins and saps in these woods resist good paint adhesion and can, in softwoods, exude from the knots and out through the finish. This problem is greatly reduced if the wood has been kiln dried.

Like most materials in nature, exposed wood suffers from the effects of abrasion caused by particulates blown in the wind or carried by human or animal activity. This form of weathering is a natural process and in many parts of the country is a desired aesthetic that bespeaks of the region, such as the New England "weathered look." Although this graying can be a desired effect, on decks, railings, and structural members, some protection may be necessary to avoid severe degradation. The weathering, or change of color, itself may not be detrimental and should not be confused with degradation. Ultraviolet radiation will change the color of a surface by causing a loosening of the wood and subsequent erosion of the surface fibers by abrasion. With temperature changes, a swelling of the wood occurs, separating the wood fibers, which are then removed by rain or wind, and over time the quality of the material can be degraded.

WOOD PRESERVATIVE TREATMENTS

In choosing materials for exterior wood construction, a number of options are available, including naturally resistant woods (cedar and redwood) and "plastic lumbers" that require less or, in the case of plastic lumber, no treatment. The use of all other common woods without treatment in exterior applications will result in rapid degradation.

The successful treatment of wood is dependent on the depth of penetration and even distribution of the solution. If the treated surface is penetrated after treatment, its effectiveness is greatly compromised. The optimum approach to prevent posttreatment penetration is to make all cuts and joints and to bore all holes before the members are treated, leaving all final surfaces exposed to treatment undisturbed. This will minimize decay, costs, and time in the field. If the members do not fit when they are delivered to the site or further holes must be bored, it is critical that a preservative be field-applied to all areas of penetration. This application, although not equal to pressure treatments (explained later in this section), will provide some protection, and with continued maintenance decay can be resisted.

The preservatives available for boards, timbers, and planking vary in chemical composition and in the type of solvent or carrier used in treatment. The treatments can be organized into three general classifications: creosote and creosote coal tar solutions, pentachlorphenol in various solutions, and waterborne salt solutions. The American Wood Preservers Institute (AWPI) has developed standards, which should be consulted in specifying a treatment. To ensure that a treated material has met these standards, a stamp or tag of the ALSC accredited inspection agency will appear on the material. With the exception of copper naphthenate, most of the most effective preservatives are classified as restricted-use pesticides, and can be used only by licensed applicators.

Oil treatments, used for hardwood and softwood structural components, are avialable in three common solutions: coal tar (creosote), which is insoluble in water and used for severe conditions; pentachlorophenol, also insoluble in water, and copper naphthenate, which is dissolvable in water. Creosote, derived from coal tar, provides a long working life span for wood in exposed situations and was once quite common. Its use has declined, however, owing to restrictions on handling and because, once installed, the chemicals are prone to leaching into the surrounding soils or water. The chemical pentachlorophenol, derived from synthetic pesticides, is restricted because the EPA has placed limits on the permissible levels of dioxins. Pentachlorophenol is not allowed for marine applications, and is permitted only in limited aboveground use. The most practical oil-based preservative, copper naphthenate, is not a restricted pesticide and is considered environmentally safe, but this treatment is the most expensive. Other waterborne treatments approved by the EPA and used by commercial treatment plants include ammoniacal copper zinc arsenate (ACZA), ammoniacal copper quaternary ammonium (ACQ) and chromated copper arsenate (CCA). These preservative chemicals are registered by the EPA as pesticides and should be applied only by treaters holding official pesticide applicators licenses. CCA has an advantage in that the chromium oxides bond to wood, decreasing photodegradation. When used beneath a transparent stain, these waterborne applications can increase durability by a factor of 2 to 3 (McDonald et al., 1996, 72).

Factory-treated wood is commonly used for all aboveground structural members and all members in contact with the ground and is often used for decking, rails, and overhead structures in outdoor applications. In situations where hand contact is expected, such as rail caps, balustrades, and seating, some treatments may not be advisable, and if the leaching of chemicals is suspected, treated wood should not be used in these applications. Many designers choose to use cedar or other naturally resistant species in situations where hand contact is probable or if the wood is used near areas where produce or herbs are being raised (i.e., where the toxins can be absorbed by the plants and there is a potential health hazard if ingested).

In the treatment plant the wood is placed in large cylindrical tanks, and the pressure in the chamber forces the preservative medium into the wood fibers, hence the term *pressure-treated wood*. The depth of penetration depends on the species, moisture content, and grade of wood. Wood species are selected both for their ability to absorb the treatment and according to regional availability. In the South, southern yellow pine is commonly used, and in the Northwest, Douglas fir and western hemlock are readily available. For species with characteristics that thwart the absorption process, such as Douglas fir, incising is used. The process consists of stamping small holes into the wood surface, allowing the chemical to penetrate evenly and saturate the wood fibers below the surface. The results of the incisement process are observable and may not be aesthetically appropriate for wood used as decking or in highly visible situations.

There is some preliminary evidence that wood treated with CCA, AZCA, or other preservatives can leach, particularly under acidic conditions. This is clearly a concern in ecologically sensitive areas, such as marshes and wetlands, and where children have contact with either the wood or the soils below. Test data, although not extensive, indicate relatively high levels of arsenic in soils directly below treated structures. There is some evidence that sealers and coatings may reduce the degree of leaching. The EPA has restricted the use of some preservatives; however, CCA and ACZA are not restricted. The Forest Products Laboratory is currently conducting further tests.

There is a new generation of chemical preservative mixes that contain no chromium or arsenic and cost as little as 5% more than standard treatments. Although they appear successful in penetrating and protecting against fungi and insects, they have not been in service long enough to be compared in performance or environmental impact with the traditional treatments. Ammoniacal copper citrate (CC) provides greater penetration than CCA and is good for treating some species difficult to treat. Alkaline copper quarternary compounds are of two types: ACQ-B and ACQ-D. ACQ-B gives greater penetration, and ACQ-D provides superior appearance. Copper dimethyldithiocarbamate (CDDC) involves a two-treatment process and does not penetrate difficult species as well as ACQ or CCA. Some of these treatments may be difficult to find in some parts of the country.

RELATED SPECIFICATIONS
06300 — Wood Treatment

MECHANICAL FASTENERS AND CONNECTORS

There is an almost staggering range of fasteners and connectors designed for attaching wood members to each other or to other materials. The decision as to which one to select is critical because these connectors provide resistance to the forces that could cause a structure to fail. The type, finish, and installation methods affect the longevity and performance in the field. Metal fasteners designed for wood construction differ in material composition, design, and function. Once the structural members are sized for their load-bearing capacity and stresses, the addition of an improper fastener can compromise the integrity of the structure. The most commonly used fasteners include nails, screws, lag screws, and bolts. Within these categories are many types designed for different applications; however, most are made from mild steel, with various galvanized finishes applied for exterior uses. At nearly triple the cost, most standard fasteners are also available in stainless steel, which provides the greatest durability.

In using any metal-to-metal connection—fasteners in contact with a connector or fasteners in contact with a roofing or flashing material, for example—the effects that can result from galvanic corrosion are always a concern. This process can occur when two different metals come in contact with each other. Galvanic corrosion is effected when a solution, most frequently water (condensation), in which the contaminants act as electrolytes, is present with two metals, and the more anodic of the metals corrodes and its material is deposited on the cathodic (more noble) metal. The process is most common in industrial and seacoast environments with increased amounts of contaminants and/or moisture. The following steps offer the best prevention:

1. Use metals that are most compatible in the galvanic series.
2. Use sacrificial coatings that are intended to corrode, leaving deposits that form a layer between the metals protecting the cathode.
3. Provide a barrier, such as paint, to protect against moisture.
4. Apply a metallic cladding onto one of the metals for compatibility—for example, copper-plated steel nails for attaching copper flashing.
5. Apply a chemical that changes the surface metal or includes an alkaline solution that reduces galvanic action.

GALVANIC SERIES OF METALS:

1. Aluminum
2. Zinc
3. Steel
4. Iron
5. Nickel
6. Tin
7. Lead
8. Copper
9. Stainless Steel

Any two metals in contact with one another in the presence of moisture will result in galvanic corrosion. The one lower on the list will cause the other to be corroded. The further apart on the list the materials are, the more rapid and corrosive the galvanic action.

Adapted from Time Saver Standards, C. Harris and N. Dines (New York: McGraw-Hill, 1988).

NAILS

Nailing serves two purposes: first, to attach two pieces of material to each other, and second, to transfer the loads from one member to another. The integrity of a nailed connection is dependent on the thickness and density of material, the type and size of the nail used, and the moisture and humidity levels to which the connection will be exposed. There is a wide selection of nails available designed for corrosion resistance and for various applications including framing, finish work, roofing, and embedment in concrete. Steel nails come in many finishes; two bright types, and those with galvanized coatings are the most common. However, steel nails are also available with cement and adhesive coatings. Bright nails are designed exclusively for interior use and will corrode immediately if used in exposed exterior situations. The bright nails will discolor many woods, including redwood and western red cedar, both of which contain natural chemicals that react to the metal, first blackening the wood and then decomposing the metal. In preservative-treated woods, the high salt content can corrode uncoated steel nails. It is critical that galvanized coated nails, at a minimum, or stainless steel nails be used in all exterior applications. Galvanized nails are available either electroplated or with hot-dipped or mechanically applied coatings. The hot dipping and mechanical application processes tend to deposit more zinc and generally produce more durable coatings than electroplating. The galvanizing is essentially a sacrificial coating; thus, the more zinc, the longer the resistance of the steel structure to corrosion.

Aluminum, brass, and copper nails are available, but in structural situations they may not provide adequate strength. However, these materials do prevent galvanic corrosion, the action that takes place between incompatible materials in the presence of moisture, whereby one of the metals fails. Therefore, such nails may be necessary in securing aluminum or copper flashing, a situation in which a steel nail would cause galvanic failure.

Nails are commonly available with two types of heads and a variety of shanks, each designed for an intended purpose. Nails with a flat circular head are called "common" nails; those with a very narrow head, resembling a slight bulge at the top, are "finish" nails. Common nails are designed for attaching structural members or for decking, and the head is driven into the member until it sits flush with the surface of the wood. Finish nails are used to attach trim boards, moldings, and other finish boards to a structural member or to each other, often in very visible applications. A finish nail head is intended to sit slightly below the surface of the wood and is often "countersunk" with a nail punch. The hole is then filled with a putty, color matched to the color of the surrounding wood. The head is much narrower than that of the common nail and is designed to penetrate the surface, leaving a small hole and minimizing the crushing of the surrounding wood fibers. Finish nails are not designed for structural applications. Both types of nails are available in a variety of lengths that are proportioned to the shank diameters. Regardless of their head or wire type (shank), nails are standardized by length based on the intended usage. The common terminology for specifying nails uses a numerical reference followed by the word *penny*, which is indicated by the letter "d." The available sizes range from 2d, proceeding in single d increments up to 10d, then in two d increments up to 20d, followed by ten d increments to 60d. Nails larger than 60d are considered "spikes" and are specified by inches in length (see Figure 2.8).

In exterior decking situations, with the frequent expansion and contraction of wood, smooth shank nails tend to loose their holding ability. The use of deformed shank nails, either spirally grooved (screw-shank) or annular grooved (ring-shank) nails are recommended to resist the tendency to loosen and withdraw. If the decking is subject to substantial saturation of moisture and fluctuations in temperature, high-quality galvanized screw-shank or stainless steel nails should be used.

Nail Chart

Trade Names	Length in Inches	Size of Material	Wire Gauge
2d	1"	Trim	15
3d	1 1/4"	Trim	14
4d	1 1/2"	Trim & Siding	12 1/2
5d	1 3/4"	Trim & Siding	12 1/2
6d	2"	Trim & Siding	11 1/2
7d	2 1/4"	Trim & Siding	11 1/2
8d	2 1/2"	1 x Material	10 1/4
9d	2 3/4"	1 x Material	10 1/4
10d	3"	2 x Material	9
12d	3 1/4"	2 x Material	9
16d	3 1/2"	2 x Material	8
20d	4"	2 x Material	6
30d	4 1/2"	2 x Material	7
40d	5"	3 x Material	7 or 5 1/2
50d	5 1/2"	3 x Material	7 or 5 1/2
60d	6"	3 x Material	7 or 5 1/2
70d	7"	3 x Material	7 or 5 1/2
80d	8"	4 x Material	5 1/2

Figure 2.8   Trade names and sizes of standard nails. *Source:* Adapted from Maze Nail, "Nails for Exterior Applications."

To determine the proper nail for any given situation, an allowable load chart should be consulted. Such charts are available from a variety of sources, including the *Western Woods Use Book*, 1973 edition, and *Landscape Architecture Construction,* H. Landphair and F. Klatt, 2nd edition, 1988.

Many builders are now, with greater frequency, using pneumatic nail guns to attach wood members. Collated nails, attached in strips, are fed into the nailer. Nailers are designed to drive either common or finish nails, and capability is based on the size of nail. The nails are available in all sizes up to 20d and come in bright or galvanized finish. Some have special coatings, usually a glue that increases adhesion between the wood members.

In addition to common and finish nails, there are many specialty nails available. These are designed for specific applications, including concrete nails (cut nails), designed to penetrate concrete; roofing nails in both galvanized and copper finishes; and duplex nails (staging nails) with double heads, designed for easy removal and particularly useful for temporary structures such as form work and temporary scaffolding.

SCREWS

Like nails, wood screws are specified according to their head and shank design, composition, finish, and size. They are available in many lengths with sizes ranging from 1¼ in. up to 3½ in., for use in attaching standard dimensioned boards. Not long ago the choice was limited to wood screws of slotted brass or steel and blackened drywall screws, neither designed for exterior applications. Today there are many options for bugle-headed screw fasteners, with both Phillips and square recessed heads and threaded shanks, designed for fast driving and with excellent holding power. The many choices of coated screws for exterior use include hot-dipped galvanized, stainless steel, and epoxy coated. In attaching woods such as cedar and redwood, stainless steel provides excellent corrosion resistance in the presence of tannic acids and other extractives found in these woods.

With the availability of screws designed for exterior uses, many designers are now specifying screws for attaching most wood members, including decking, roofing, balustrades, and the like. The number of fasteners needed per square foot of decking is available in manufacturers' guides.

LAG SCREWS AND BOLTS

Lag screws, although technically screws, function as bolts. They have large shank diameters and are used to connect large structural wood members. A lag screw is essentially a point-threaded shank with a hex head on the opposite end. Lag screws are used when other options, such as access to drill a through hole for a carriage bolt, are not possible. For example, lag bolts are often used to attach a ledger (2 × 6 or larger) to a rim joist (double joists that are mechanically fastened at the perimeter of the structure) where access to the rim joist is not possible. In specifying lag screws, it must be remembered that at least half the length of the screw should penetrate the second member to which the first member is being attached. A washer with hole diameter no greater than ⅛ in. of the lag screw shank should be used so as to avoid crushing the wood fibers at the screw head. Lag screws and carriage and machine bolts are available with hot-dipped galvanized coatings or in stainless steel for exterior use (see Figure 2.9).

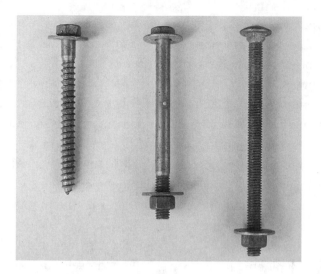

Figure 2.9 Bolt and screw types: *(left)* lag screw; *(middle)* machine bolt with nut and washers; *(right)* carriage bolt with nut and washer.

Both carriage and hexagonal-head machine bolts are threaded at one end to receive nuts and washers. A carriage bolt has a round head, and a machine bolt a hexagonal (hex) head. A machine bolt can be tightened at each end by turning both the hex head and the nut. The carriage bolt relies on applied pressure to the round head, immobilizing the shank so the nut can be tightened. Both require a predrilled hole no more than $\frac{1}{16}$ in. larger than the bolt shaft, through all connecting wood members. After drilling, the hole should be saturated with a preservative before the bolts are inserted. Both types of bolt require washers on the nut and head ends to avoid crushing the wood and marring the appearance. Charts specifying the number of bolts or lag screws required to attach specific members are available from manufacturers and in structural engineering books (see Figure 2.10).

Joist spacing		Joist span		
		0–6 ft	**6–12 ft**	**12–16 ft**
40 lb/ft²	12 in.	(2) – 3/8 in. @ 24 in.	(2) – 1/2 in. @ 24 in.	(2) – 1/2 in. @ 24 in.
	16 in.	(2) – 3/8 in. @ 24 in.	(2) – 1/2 in. @ 24 in.	(2) – 1/2 in. @ 24 in.
	24 in.	(2) – 3/8 in. @ 24 in.	(2) – 1/2 in. @ 24 in.	(2) – 1/2 in. @ 24 in.
60 lb/ft²	12 in.	(2) – 3/8 in. @ 24 in.	(2) – 1/2 in. @ 24 in.	(2) – 1/2 in. @ 18 in.
	16 in.	(2) – 3/8 in. @ 16 in.	(2) – 1/2 in. @ 16 in.	(2) – 1/2 in. @ 16 in.
	24 in.	(2) – 1/2 in. @ 24 in.	(2) – 5/8 in. @ 24 in.	(2) – 5/8 in. @ 20 in.

Number of lag screws or bolts given in parentheses.

Figure 2.10 Recommended number, diameter, and spacing of lag screws or bolts for attaching deck to a house. *Source:* K. A. McDonald, R. F. Falk, R. S. Williams, and J. E. Winandy, *Wood Decks, Materials, Construction and Finishing* (Madison, Wisconsin: USDA, 1996).

For appearance and safety purposes it is common to "countersink" bolt heads. This is done by preboring a hole, ½ to ⅝ in., that is ⅛ in. greater than the washer being used, into exterior surface of the members that will be visible. The through hole is bored into the center of this hole. The first hole enables the nut, washer, and bolt end to sit below the surface of the material. This is important if the structure is near pedestrian traffic or is a piece of play equipment because a protruding nut and bolt end can cause physical harm. Bolts are also countersunk to create a refined appearance. After the nut is inserted and tightened, a wooden dowel (plug) is cut, glued, inserted into the hole, and sanded flush with the surface, covering the nut and washer and blending into the surrounding wood.

In choosing a fastener, its ability to resist corrosion and withdrawal is a primary consideration. As the wood shrinks and swells, improperly specified fasteners can loosen and withdraw from the wood members, causing structural failure. In certain environments, where warm temperatures and high humidity (southeastern states) coexist with salt spray, rapid corrosion will result. Stainless steel is a cost-effective solution; AISI Grade 316 stainless steel provides the greatest corrosion resistance in saline conditions.

RELATED SPECIFICATIONS
05030 — Metal Coatings
06050 — Fasteners and Adhesives

WOOD CONNECTORS

Wood connectors can be divided into five primary groups defined by use: concrete; caps and bases; hangers, straps, and ties; miscellaneous; and options. The standard connectors are available in several types of galvanized coatings and in stainless steel. The hot-dipped galvanized or triple zinc-coated (three times the zinc in the hot-dipped galvanized) require galvanized fasteners and washers; stainless connectors require stainless steel washers and nuts.

CONCRETE CONNECTORS

Concrete connectors are designed to attach wood members to concrete foundation walls, footings, slabs, or pilasters. Most are designed to tie a mud sill (a 2× wood member bolted to the top of a foundation wall) to receive joists or beam, although anchors are available to fasten beams, girders, and trusses to a foundation or footing. Concrete connectors can be divided into two groups, designed for different applications: retrofit bolts and embedment anchors. Retrofit bolts are designed to be set and bonded to a masonry structure in a predrilled hole. These are used in situations where wood members must be attached to an existing concrete or masonry vertical wall or horizontal surface. They are commonly used in renovations, replacing rotted members, and for deck additions. The bolts are bonded to the concrete with the use of two-part epoxy adhesives or nonshrink cementitious grouts. Because (retrofit) bolt anchors are installed after the pour, they can be laid out and drilled on an existing structure after the form has been stripped; thus, close tolerances are easily achieved.

The second group includes anchor bolts and hold-downs which are set in place during the concrete pour and are embedded into the cured form. When these connectors are installed, the layout must be highly accurate because once embedded, their position is fixed. Anchor bolts are vertically extended out from the concrete, with the threaded end rising through a wood member or metal connector to receive a nut and washer; thus, the wood member is bolted flush to the concrete foundation. Hold-downs are not bolts but consist of brackets, hurricane ties, or strap connections. One advantage of the embedded anchors over bolted connections is that the embedded portion of the hold-down is deformed (bent at an angle or curve), providing strong resistance to withdrawal once set (see Figure 2.11 B).

POST CAPS AND BASES

Base anchors are designed to be either embedded or epoxied into a concrete form or to be bolted to another wood member. They are available as either fixed or adjustable anchors and are designed to receive standard vertical posts, ranging in size from 4 × 4 in. to 12 × 12 in. Once the base anchor is embedded or bolted, the wood post is set into the steel form, holes are drilled, and machine bolts are used to form the connection. The caps make up a series of connectors designed to sit on top of a post or column and provide a seat to receive a horizontal member (beam or joist) above. Each connection is prebored to receive carriage bolts and/or screws or nails for the post and the horizontal member. The maximum loads are given in suppliers' catalogs (see Figure 2.11 A).

HANGERS

Hangers are of two types: face mount and top flange hangers. Both are designed to connect a horizontal member (beam or joist) with another horizontal member (beam). A face mount hanger is connected into the face of the

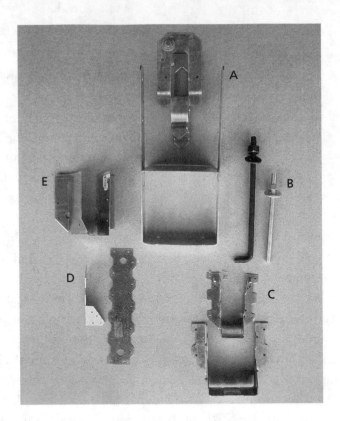

Figure 2.11 Examples of connectors from each of the five categories, beginning clockwise from the top: A: post bases, B: anchor and retrofit bolts, C: joist hangers, D: flat and twist straps, and E: special option angled joist hanger.

supporting member, and a top flange hanger is attached to the top of the supporting member, bending 90 degrees down the face to receive the supported member. Both are available with preset 45-degree horizontal angles, and other angles can be specified. They rely on nails, screws, or bolts to form the connection (see Figure 2.11 C).

STRAPS AND TIES

Straps and ties are used to form a mechanical tie between two wood members, eliminating tow or end nailing and increasing the rigidity of the joint especially in areas prone to seismic activity. Included in this category are seismic and hurricane ties, framing anchors, and strap ties (see Figure 2.11 D).

MISCELLANEOUS AND HANGER OPTIONS

The miscellaneous category includes a variety of bases, fence brackets, header hangers, twist straps (to attach a joist seated on a beam), wall bracing, bridging, and other devices.

The hanger options category includes hangers designed to receive multiple members (joists or rafters) with preset angles. Also included in this category are custom hangers and connectors for applications in which a steel plate is cut, bent, and has predrilled holes, as designated by a computer-aided design (see Figure 2.11 E).

For sizing purposes, most manufacturers, including Simpson Strong-Tie, provide data for calculating uplift, allowable bearing, and lateral loads for the available connectors.

COATINGS FOR FASTENERS AND CONNECTORS

Fasteners and connectors are available with a galvanized coating or can be treated with paint, plastic, or metal coatings to resist corrosion. The mild steel used in noncoated fasteners or connectors is not intended for exterior use. When exposed to the elements, it will rust and stain the surrounding wood and is prone to rapid corrosion, thus weakening the strength of the material and in time resulting in structural failure.

The most common form of treatment is galvanic, whereby a zinc-cadmium coating is applied to the steel. The metallic coating is applied by electroplating, mechanical plating, chemical treating, or hot dipping (molten zinc). The hot dipping method produces the coating with the thickest profile, and research has shown that provides the greatest longevity and resistance to corrosion.

The thickness of a galvanized coating is of particular concern when used with CCA or ACZA pressure-treated lumber in below-grade applications. The copper salts used in the waterborne preservatives act as a copper cathode, which, through electrolytic action, attacks and corrodes the "sacrificial" (galvanized) coating. Proceeding unchecked, the corrosion will continue to the steel connector itself. To prolong the life of a structure in warm and damp areas prone to high corrosion, the galvanized coating should be applied at a thickness of >1.0 oz/sq ft.

In situations where salt is airborne, or in marine applications, stainless steel is a better choice than hot-dipped galvanized fasteners or connectors. Research has shown little long-term degradation of stainless steel in the most disadvantageous conditions.

Aluminum fasteners are another option; however, research has shown that when in contact with treated lumber they are particularly susceptible to corrosion and should be avoided in such situations.

It is recommended that when fastening or using connectors on treated or naturally decay-resistant wood in above-grade situations, hot-dipped galva-

RELATED SPECIFICATIONS
06050—Fasteners and
Adhesives

nized steel fasteners with at least 0.85 oz of zinc per sq. ft be used (McDonald et al., 1996, 42). For wood below grade or exposed to saline conditions, stainless steel fasteners of Grade 304, minimum, are recommended.

ADHESIVES

The use of mechanical fasteners to join wood has many applications; however, some situations require extra or different means of joining, for which an adhesive may be suitable. In gluing laminated beams or blocks for turning, or in attaching finials or moldings, adhesives can provide a strong connection more easily and effectively than either nails or screws. Adhesives achieve their strength through the combination of two systems. First, a mechanical connection is formed as tiny tendrils of glue penetrate the surface structure of the wood faces, creating a bond. A second means of adhesion results from a molecular attraction between the adhesive and the wood (Herbertson, 1991, 40).

There are several reasons that a bond may not be achievable with the use of adhesives: The adhesive may be incompatible with the material to be bonded, the material may have a moisture content that is too high, the ambient temperature may be beyond the range of the adhesives and the surfaces may not be clean.

Glues based on resorcinol-formaldehyde and phenol-resorcinol-formaldehyde are formulated for exterior applications. Often called "waterproof" glues, these glues are very strong and have become the standard for glue-laminated structural members. Resorcinol and resorcinol-formaldehyde glues are ideal for bonding high-density hardwoods such as oak. Phenol-resorcinol-formaldehydes are less expensive than resorcinol-formaldehydes and have similar curing characteristics, pot and shelf life, and temperature requirements; these are commonly used to structurally bond softwoods. Their long pot life—3¾ hours—make these glues a good choice for situations involving considerable clamping and assembly. The resorcinol-formaldehydes require curing temperatures of at least 70°F, and their use in colder climates can be limited. When the liquid resin is mixed with the powdered hardener, a dark red glue is produced, which may not be acceptable in certain finish applications.

All resorcinol glues require closely mated surfaces for effective bonding, with hardwoods requiring clamping pressures as high as 250 psi and softwoods 100 to 125 psi. These pressures force the glue over the wood surface and into the wood cell structure. The optimum strength is achieved in woods with a moisture content between 6 and 12%. Caution should be used when working with either resorcinol-formaldehyde or phenol-resorcinol- formaldehyde, as both are toxic in their uncured states.

Epoxies are among the most versatile and expensive of the adhesives. They have multiple applications, including anchoring concrete and masonry fasteners and restoring rotting wood. Inactive until combined, the two-part formula consists of a resin (epichlorohydrin and Bisphenol A) that is mixed with a curing agent (polyamine) to begin the setting of the glue. Other curing agents designed for different working characteristics, mechanical properties, and durability can be added.

The curing of epoxies is achieved through exothermic (heat-generated) polymerization reaction. The cured bonding agent is resistant to heat and to most corrosive agents (Herbertson, 1991, 43).

Evidence has shown that structural epoxy bonds in members subject to prolonged outdoor exposure and water saturation can deteriorate rapidly; however, some early research suggests that priming with a 2% solution of polyethyleneamine may improve exterior performance. In situations with high moisture contents, resorcinol may be a better choice if the bonded members are to be exposed.

Polyurethane foams are commonly used as insulating sealants; however, foam adhesives offer many benefits and, depending on the formulation, can bond either wet or frozen, treated or untreated lumber. These adhesives are nontoxic, waterproof, and temperature tolerant. Most of the foam glues are applied with aerosol containers and consist of isocyanates and polyol resins; some environmentally conscious manufacturers are using a benign nitrogen gas as the propellant. Available since 1972, Gorilla glue is a polyurethane glue that is applied from a bottle. The designated working time is 20 minutes, although the members can be moved for up to 45 minutes. Gorilla glue reaches a 90% complete cure within four hours at a room temperature of 68°F. The glue, once cured, is waterproof, and because curing is triggered by the moisture in the air or the material to be bonded, it will activate on wood with a moisture content of up to 25%. The glue is 100% solvent free and emits only trace amounts of CO_2. When cured, Gorilla glue is sandable and stainable.

Gorilla glue is not recommended for use in temperatures below 40°F. It dries to an amber color, so any residual glue should be removed with denatured alcohol or a solvent. Polyurethane foams tend to be costly, but the extended working life provided and their ability to withstand exterior conditions may warrant the increased costs.

RELATED SPECIFICATIONS
06050—Fasteners and Adhesives

Figure 3.17   At the midpoint of this boxed column, a louvered vent facilitates air circulation between the structural member and the boxed post, allowing moisture to escape.

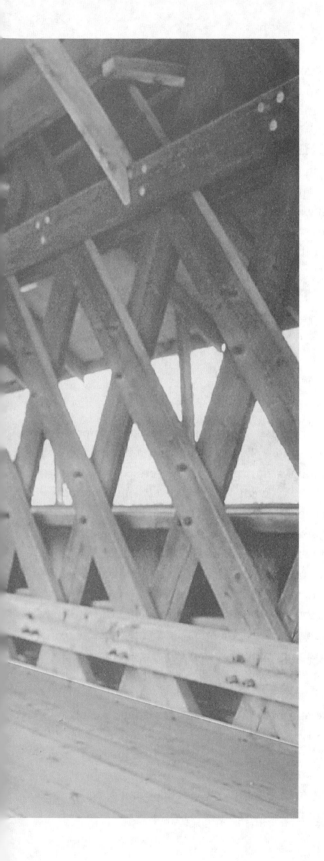

3
CONSTRUCTION METHODOLOGIES

This chapter offers a description of the wood construction methodologies used to build the structures that are typically designed by landscape architects. Many structures, such as site amenities, paving, and play structures, have not been included, owing, in part, to the limited scope of this book. However, the concepts, details, and illustrations provided in this chapter can serve and inform design methodologies for these and similar structures in the reader's design studies or practice.

A number of general concepts apply in any construction with wood in the landscape. Moisture buildup, penetration, and the associated damaged caused by fungi, mold, and insects, are the most frequent causes of wood failure. As discussed in Chapter 2, it is important to be knowledgeable about preservative treatments, their applications, and their effectiveness and limitations in preventing moisture penetration and insect infestation. Despite the benefits of pressure-treated wood, inappropriate detailing and joinery, particularly that which requires on-site cutting and penetration of the outer surface, defeats the effectiveness of the treatment. An understanding of the materials, combined with a fundamental knowledge of construction detailing, is critical to the successful design of lasting structures in the landscape.

In detailing a wood construction the first rule is to drain all water away from the structure. Slope finish grades away from the post connections, and provide positive drainage within the structure for decks, stairs, and landings. All deck railings, fence caps, and horizontal surfaces should be pitched to drain, and all water must be directed away from a joint's exposed end grain. In detailing structures, all framing should be raised off the ground to allow adequate air circulation between and below the wood members. If possible, prevent roof runoff from splashing against the wall surfaces by extending the eaves 18 in. out and by starting wood construction 12 in. above the finish grade, which will help to protect the lower wood cladding, trim, and framing. Corners, depressions, and joints prone to water or snow collection should be avoided. Details that maximize air circulation, avoid water collection points, and protect end grain surfaces will prolong the life span of the structure.

STRUCTURES

Wood structures must be designed to resist the stresses of tensile, compressive, and lateral forces acting upon them. These three forces are accounted for in the design process in selecting, sizing, placing, and connecting wood members. The process of structurally composing routinely encountered fences, gates, decks, arbors, and gazebos is relatively straightforward. An example of this process follows, showing the structural calculations for a deck using standard charts and tables (see pages 60–63). For larger decks, small pavilions, and bridges, the applied forces may be more significant and complex, requiring the consultation of a structural engineer.

Compressive forces, such as those applied by a load above down onto a column or post, tend to shorten the wood member and can cause it to buckle. The wood fibers in a post supporting a beam compress as the post resists the weight transferred from the beam. A tensile force tends to stretch the bearing member. For example, jumping on a trampoline causes the material to lengthen as the forces are applied. At midspan a horizontal member undergoes both compression above and tension below (see Figure 3.1). The third type, lateral force, is applied perpendicularly to a vertical member. In exterior structures lateral forces are typically the wind loads borne by the vertical members. Forces are measured in terms of weight per unit of area, in pounds per square foot (psf) or in pounds per square inch (psi).

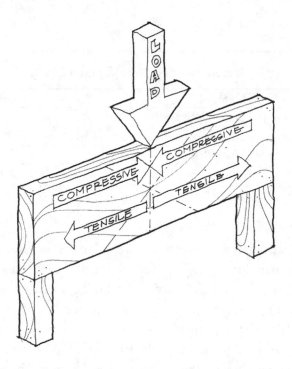

Figure 3.1   For a structure to stand, it must be sized to resist the forces of tension and compression. *Source:* Illustration by Jody Estes.

Loads on a structure can be calculated as dead or live loads. A dead load is the weight of the materials composing the structure, fixtures, and any other elements that are permanently attached to the structure. Live loads are all nonpermanent objects that will use, or bear on, the structure, including people, furniture, plants, water, and the like.

Span and height tables are often used as the most expedient means of sizing structural members. These tables are available from several agencies, including the United States Department of Agriculture (USDA) and the National Association of Forest and Paper Products. Most of the charts are based on structural lumber with a grading of No. 2 or better and are divided by species or species group and clustered by cross-sectional strength capabilities. Tables are available to determine post heights and beam, joist, and decking spans. In using the listed maximum spans, the wood member must be without flaws, including checks and knots, inasmuch as any structural flaws may compromise the calculations. Structural engineers typically include a safety factor, often 15%, and it is common practice to choose spans below the capable maximum. The tables are based on either maximum loads of 50 psf, which include a live load of 40 psf and dead load of 10 psf, or a combined load of 60 lb, using a 10 psf dead load. Most situations will be accommodated in this range of loads. In determining the concentrated loads of some structures (hot tubs, for example), additional calculations will be required (see Figure 3.2).

Figure 3.2

Recommended Decking Live Loads	
Material	Load. lb/ft^2
Residential decks, light traffic	40
Public decks, heavy traffic	80–100
Pedestrian Bridges	100
Vehicular Bridges, light traffic	200–300

Adapted from U.S.D.A. Construction Guides for Exposed Decks, U.S.D.A.Handbook No. 432, 1972.

The process of sizing most structures is carried out from top to bottom. In a covered structure, sizing begins with the roof, and span charts are available for rafters. With a deck or pedestrian bridge, sizing begins with the deck boards, moving down through the joists, to the beams, and down to the posts. Although the working process appears to be linear, it is in fact a circular one. After the initial design of the structure, the look may not be satisfying and can be changed by revisiting the spacing, spans, and material dimensions of the wood members until suitable properties and character are achieved. Footings, calculated by the tributary load method, are discussed on pages 104–105.

DECKING SPANS

Sizing for a deck begins with the uppermost members, at the floor of the deck, with the decking boards. Recommended lumber dimensions for decking include ⁵⁄₄ ×6 radius edged boards, 2 × 4, and 2 × 6. For a single decking member, the span of the board is the distance in length it can go from joist to joist or from bearing point to bearing point. Deck span tables can be consulted. Figure 3.3 provides a recommended span of 24 in. for a Southern pine 2 × 4. The U.S. Department of Agriculture tables provide maximum spans that are substantially greater, 16 in. for ⁵⁄₄ × 6 and 24 in. for 2 × 4s and 2 × 6s. Specific design configurations may require smaller spans that are acceptable. Smaller decking spans condense the spacing of the joists, increasing the amount of lumber and the weight of the deck to be supported. Once the decking material span and its equivalent joist spacing are selected, the joist size and span can be determined. A wider than recommended deck span can cause the deck boards to bounce under load, resulting in failure of the boards or the fasteners.

Figure 3.3

Maximum Spans for Decking		
Species Group	Decking Material	Recommended Span
Douglas-fir,	RED (5/4" Radius Edge Decking)	16"
Southern pine,		
Hem-Fir,		
Southern pine-Fir	2X4	24"
Ponderosa pine,		
Redwood,		
Western cedar	2X6	24"

Adapted from U.S.D.A. Forest Services Labratory, 1996.

JOIST SPANS

The span of a joist, the distance between the two bearing points of the beams, is also the beam spacing. To determine this distance, consult Figure 3.4. Several standard joist sizes are indicated, 2 × 6 to 2 × 10, and charts are available for 2 × 12s, although joists of this size are rarely needed. The joist spacing given in the table, 12 in., 16 in., and 24 in., are also standard and

Figure 3.4

Maximum Spans for Joists: 40lb/ft design load				
Species Group	Decking Material	Recommended Span		
		12"	16"	24"
Douglas fir,	2x6	10' 4"	9' 7"	7' 10"
Southern pine	2x8	13' 8"	12' 7"	10' 4"
	2x10	17' 5"	15' 11"	12' 11"
	2x12	20' 0"	17' 10"	14' 7"
Hem-Fir,	2x6	9' 2"	8' 5"	7' 1"
Southern pine-Fir	2x8	12' 1"	11' 1"	9' 4"
	2x10	15' 4"	14' 3"	11' 8"
	2x12	18' 8"	17' 10"	13' 6"
Ponderosa pine,	2x6	8' 10"	7' 11"	6' 7"
Redwood,	2x8	11' 8"	10' 4"	8' 5"
Western cedar	2x10	14' 10"	13' 2"	10' 7"
	2x12	17' 9"	17' 10"	12' 7"

Adapted from U.S.D.A. Forest Services Labratory, 1996 and U.S.D.A. Construction Guides for Exposed Decks, U.S.D.A. Handbook No. 432, 1972.

should be matched as closely as possible to the chosen decking spans. Once the joist size, spacing, and species are selected, the joist span and the equivalent beam spacing will be indicated.

BEAM SPANS

With the beam spacing in hand, Figure 3.5 can be consulted to choose the size and span of a beam. The span of the beam will be its length between the two bearing points of the posts. Standard beam sizes ranging from 4 × 6 to 6 × 12 are shown for selected species. Built-up beams may require further calculations because they vary in deflection and in their ability to resist forces. If the design calls for closely spaced beams, two members laid parallel without internal blocking, the members act independently and should be calculated using the dimensions of the single member. For example, two 2 × 10 beams sandwiched to posts have the span capacity of a single 2 × 10.

Figure 3.5

Maximum Spans for Beams: 40lb/ft design load											
Species Group	Beam Material	Beam Spacing									
		4'	5'	6'	7'	8'	9'	10'	11'	12'
Douglas fir,	4x6	7'	7'	6'						
Southern pine	4x8	10'	9'	8'	7'	7'	6'	6'	6'	
	4x10	12'	11'	10'	9'	8'	8'	7'	7'	7'
	4x12	14'	13'	11'	11'	10'	9'	9'	8'	8'
	6x10	15'	13'	12'	12'	11'	10'	9'	9'	8'
	6x12	16'	16'	15'	13'	12'	12'	11'	10'	10'
Hem-Fir,	4x6	7'	6'							
Southern pine-Fir	4x8	8'	7'	6'	6'					
	4x10	11'	10'	9'	8'	7'	7'	6'	6'	
	4x12	13'	12'	10'	10'	9'	9'	8'	8'	7'
	6x10	12'	12'	11'	10'	10'	9'	9'	8'	8'
	6x12	15'	13'	12'	12'	11'	11'	10'	9'	9'
Ponderosa pine,	4x6	6'								
Redwood,	4x8	8'	7'	6'	6'					
Western cedar	4x10	10'	9'	8'	8'	7'	7'	6'	6'	6'
	4x12	12'	11'	10'	9'	9'	8'	8'	7'	7'
	6x10	12'	12'	11'	10'	9'	9'	8'	8'	8'
	6x12	15'	13'	12'	11'	11'	10'	9'	8'	8'

Adapted from U.S.D.A. Forest Services Labratory, 1996 and U.S.D.A. Construction Guides for Exposed Decks, U.S.D.A. Handbook No. 432, 1972.

Figure 3.6

Maximum Post Height: 40lb/ft design load										
Species Group	Post Material	Post Load Area = beam spacing x post spacing. ft²								
		36	48	60	72	84	96	108	120	132
Douglas fir,	4x4	12'	12'	11'	10'	9'	8'	8'	7'	7'
Southern pine	4x6	14'	14'	13'	12'	11'	10'	10'	9'	9'
	6x6 (#1)	17'	17'	17'	17'	17'	17'	16'	16'	16'
	6x6 (#2)	17'	17'	17'	17'	17'	16'	14'	14'	12'
Hem-Fir,	4x4	12'	12'	10'	10'	9'	9'	8'	8'	7'
Southern pine-Fir	4x6	14'	14'	12'	12'	11'	11'	10'	9'	9'
	6x6 (#1)	17'	17'	17'	17'	16'	14'	14'	12'	12'
	6x6 (#2)	17'	17'	17'	16'	15'	13'	12'	11'	11'
Ponderosa pine,	4x4	12'	10'	9'	8'	8'	7'	7'	6'	5'
Redwood,	4x6	14'	13'	12'	11'	10'	9'	8'	8'	7'
Western cedar	6x6 (#1)	17'	17'	16'	14'	14'	12'	12'	12'	12'
	6x6 (#2)	17'	16'	16'	13'	12'	12'	12'	7'	

Adapted from U.S.D.A. Forest Services Labratory, 1996 and U.S.D.A. Construction Guides for Exposed Decks, U.S.D.A. Handbook No. 432, 1972.

Internal blocking in a double beam provides increased strength and deflection, according to the amount of blocking used. A built-up beam will always have less strength and resistance than a solid member of a similar size.

POST SIZES

The final calculation for the wood structure of the deck uses a derivation of the load and a chosen height to determine the size of the post in cross section (Figure 3.6). The load, known as the tributary load, is a figure for square area calculated by multiplying the beam spacing by the post spacing. The post height is measured from the footing attachment to the post beam connection. The tributary load area and the chosen post height can be located on a post height table to give the size of post required in cross-sectional dimension. The choice of posts should be made according to appearance as well as structural integrity. A tall 4 × 4 post may look thin in comparison with a large deck, and increasing the size may provide a more pleasing proportional relationship.

FOOTING SIZES

The size of a concrete spread footing is calculated using the bearing pressure of the soils and the amount of tributary load each footing will be required to support. The bearing capacity of soils is available at the local building department and will be given as pounds per square feet (psf). To determine the tributary load of each footing, the following calculation is made. If the deck is *uniformly loaded,* the total area of deck in square feet is multiplied by the loads (for example, 50 lb psf, typical combined dead and live loads), multiplied by the total square footage of the deck and divided by the number of posts. This will provide the tributary loads carried by each post and its footing.

To determine the size of the footing, divide the load on the footing by the soil bearing capacity. For example, to determine a footing to support a post carrying an individual load of 2,000 psf with a soil bearing capacity of 1,500 psf, divide 2,000 psf by 1,500 psf, which equals 1.33 or 192 sq. in. For a square footing, this is equal to about 13¾ in. per side, thus a 14 in. × 14 in. footing will work. The same area can be computed to size a round form. It is common to reduce the size of the pier rising up from the spread, because the pier is simply transferring the load to the spread and a pier the size of the spread will be more than is necessary.

RELATED SPECIFICATIONS
03100—Concrete
    Formwork
03200—Concrete
    Reinforcement
03300—Cast-in-Place
    Concrete

FENCES

HISTORY

The use of wood members to divide and define space and create an enclosure is tied to the establishment of fixed settlements with private or communal land and domesticated animal ownership, and the physical demarcations of these spaces to form communities with rules and regulations. Nomadic hunter-gatherers had little use for fences, but once a desire for permanence was established, various versions of wood fences begin to appear both for containment, mainly for animals, and for defense against enemies. The derivation of the word "fence" is the old French word *defense,* and previously the Latin *defendere,* "to knock or strike down," hence, to protect (Nash, 1999, 7).

A very early form of post and rail wooden fencing is referenced in a farmer's treatise from 50 B.C. with a description of the bored holes in the posts and the rails thrust through the openings. The first fence type built by Europeans in the United States appears to be a pale fence, in which pointed wooden stakes (pales) were driven into the ground and lashed to a horizontal sapling or bound by a split rail at the top ends.

Uniquely American is the worm fence, also called the Virginia rail fence, zigzag fence, or the crooked rail fence, which relies solely on the combined weight of the fence members for stability. The style was popular from the late 1650s through the late 1800s, occurring in all parts of the country except in New England, where the traditional mortised post and rail fence was used. The advantages of a Virginia rail fence are its easy construction and reconfiguration. The split rails are alternately stacked, log cabin style, without posts or joinery (see Figures 3.7 A and B). The disadvantage of this method is that

Figure 3.7A One of the early fence styles, the Virginia rail or "worm fence," was easy to build but consumed large quantities of material.

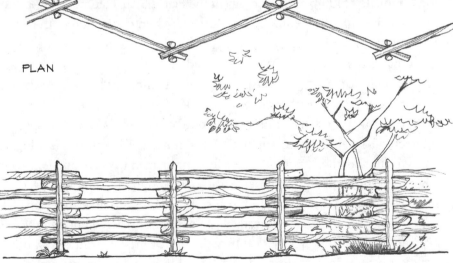

PLAN

ELEVATION

Figure 3.7B One advantage of the "worm fence" is it required no posts, saving in labor and allowing portability. The zigzagging alignment, however—designed to increase stability—took up a lot of space, and cultivation near the fence was limited. *Source:* Illustration by Jody Estes.

Figure 3.8   The shipping trade brought wealth to New England cities. Richly ornamented fences, complete with finials, detailed posts, and turned pickets, were built at the street edge, many by carpenters trained in shipbuilding.

it requires a great amount of wood. With sawmills in the mid-1600s producing board lumber, the post and board design, requiring far less material, came into favor. Lumber was also needed for boat building and was the source of fuel for home, industry, and transportation. By the 1700s, there was a growing concern that wood supplies should be conserved.

The westward migration of the mid-nineteenth century necessitated another adaptation.

While the forests of New England and the Southeast had provided prodigious amounts of lumber, the ecology of the Plains States did not. The lack of native fencing materials impeded the settlement and cultivation of the fertile soils of the plains. The West was opened to farming in large part by the invention of barbed wire fencing. With wire used in lieu of wood rails, wood was required only for posts, and large areas of ranching and crop production could be secured at a reasonable cost.

For a growing urban middle-class population, fences were a display of architectural ornament in the eighteenth and nineteenth centuries (see Figure 3.8). Wealthy Bostonians could hire master craftsmen to carve and construct elaborate posts and balustrades, extending the design of the house out to the street. Books of patterns organized by historical style, veritable encyclopedias of ornament, were commonly available sources and widely mined in the late nineteenth century. Earlier that century the front yards of farmhouses, previously left bare, were transformed into formal yards with shrubs, paths, and painted board fences. The formal order of the landscape reflected the moral order of the independent and upright farmer. By the mid-1850s the formality of the front yard was seen as being too restrained, and Andrew Jackson Downing's naturalistic approach became influential. His designs for summer estates blended house and grounds together in a picturesque manner, using rusticated fences and other garden structures. Downing helped to popularize the Gothic Revival style, and the availability of steam-powered band saws and woodworking tools made decorative millwork affordable. Some of these ornamentations were mass produced and could be picked out of catalogs; others were custom-made on-site. The Gothic revival was a primary influence on the Victorian style fences and yard ornamentation found in the urban and suburban landscapes of the time.

Fencing the front yard was seen as antisocial in late nineteenth century suburban developments. The yard was viewed as a green extension of the house and a neighborly joining of the community. Despite the intent, the social life of the family largely moved into the rear yard, and as the backyard has become an increasingly private domain, it is now secured by high, opaque, and secure fences that seem more like the early "pale fences," restraints from outsiders entering either physically or visually. In densely inhabited areas many people read fences as statements of value about neighborliness, privacy, security, style, and ornamentation (see Figure 3.9).

Figure 3.9 An urban security and privacy fence erected to the limits of code. Note the 1 × 2 nailing stop attached to the posts, and top and bottom rails to receive the vertical boards. The changing widths of the vertical members add some visual interest to this solid board fence.

Fences are available in historic and contemporary styles from specialty fence companies and commercial outlets, and "build it yourself" guides have replaced the nineteenth-century pattern books. Fences can be designed and produced using prefabricated panels and posts, standard dimensioned lumber, customized ornaments, or any hybrid of these elements. This tremendous range of styles and types of wood fences, with variations in the shape and orientation of pickets or the decorative nature of the posts, balustrades, and rails, continues to evolve; however, the basic construction methods remain similar for all.

The first considerations for fence design involve layout, where on-site the fence can and should go, and what it will look like in elevation. If the fence is a boundary fence, its layout and height will be limited by property line setbacks. Setbacks are regulated by city and county agencies having juristiction over the local building codes. Front, back, and side property lines may have differing setbacks. Function, aesthetics, topography, wind patterns, and costs are all factors in the layout. Will the fence be used to corral horses, protect children, provide privacy and security? Will the fence shape new spaces, relate to structures, pathways, and gardens? How will it align with steep topography? Are there conflicts with proposed footing locations? The footing locations will relate to the span and size of materials needed for horizontal members (see Figures 3.10 A and B).

Figures 3.10 A and B   Two alternate methods for aligning a fence on a sloping site. *Top:* Fence panels, stepped equally down the slope, are possible only if the slope maintains a consistent grade. *Bottom:* The rails, oriented with the sloping grade, result in the cutting of all vertical boards to the appropriate angle. *Source:* Illustration by Jody Estes.

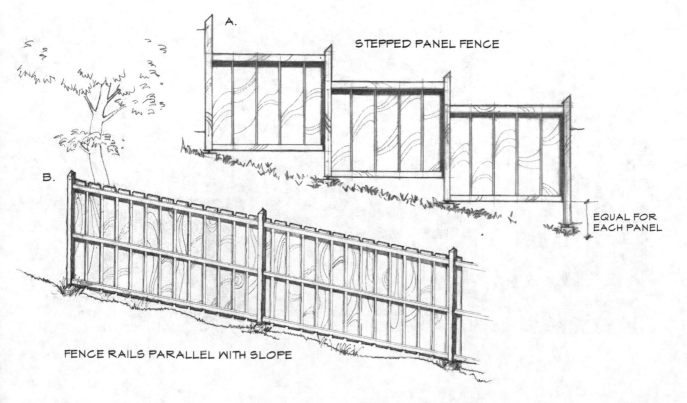

A.

STEPPED PANEL FENCE

EQUAL FOR EACH PANEL

B.

FENCE RAILS PARALLEL WITH SLOPE

A. STEP BACK PERPENDICULAR TO PROPERTY LINE

Figures 3.11 A and B A crenallated fence increases resistance to wind loads and offers visual interest and opportunities to plant vines and small trees. *Source:* Illustration by Jody Estes.

B. STEP BACK ANGLED TO PROPERTY LINE

The layout and detailing of a fence can be designed to resist and dissipate the lateral forces of wind, both extending the life of the structure and calming the site. In addition to designing for maximum wind resistance, proper detailing can extend the longevity of the materials. A straight run of any fencing is the weakest form, as it is reliant solely on the posts for wind resistance. Almost any deviation from a straight line increases resistance to lateral forces. Common repeating structures are zigzags and crenellated forms that jog from one side to the other of a center line. Each directional turn of the fence adds stability to its structure and produces angles of deflection against changeable winds. Fences of this type consume more space but can offer opportunities for planting or seating. In high-wind situations the use of slats with optimum spacing will reduce the forces on the fence, and careful detailing of louvers oriented to the prevailing winds can reduce these even further (see Figures 3.11 A and B).

POSTS

The structural integrity of any fence begins with the posts. These vertical members connect the horizontal rails and any boards they carry, and anchor this structure to the earth. The post size is determined by the height and width of the fence panels, the combined weight of the materials used, and the character desired. In most applications with a height of 6 ft or less and a width of 8 ft or less, 4 × 4 posts are adequate for stability. If the fence is higher than 6 ft, 6 × 6 timbers are recommended for corner or end posts. If heavy gates are to be mounted, the posts should be increased to 6 × 6 or greater (see Figure 3.12).

Posts, of only pressure-treated wood rated for ground contact or a naturally resistant species, may be embedded in the earth. The preferred installation is attachment to a concrete footing with a galvanized or stainless steel post anchor. Embedding a post directly into the concrete is not recommended, as concrete traps and wicks water, causing the ends of the posts to decay. The footing top should be sloped to drain so that water does not build up and infiltrate the end grain of the post (see Figure 3.13).

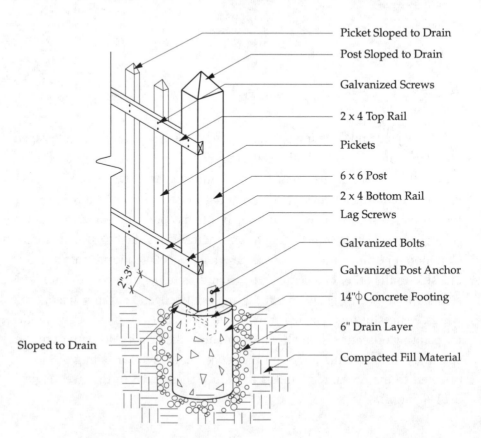

Picket Sloped to Drain

Post Sloped to Drain

Galvanized Screws

2 x 4 Top Rail

Pickets

6 x 6 Post

2 x 4 Bottom Rail

Lag Screws

Galvanized Bolts

Galvanized Post Anchor

14"φ Concrete Footing

6" Drain Layer

Compacted Fill Material

Sloped to Drain

2"-3"

Figure 3.12 Post footing connection with inset rail. *Source:* Illustration by Chad Wichers.

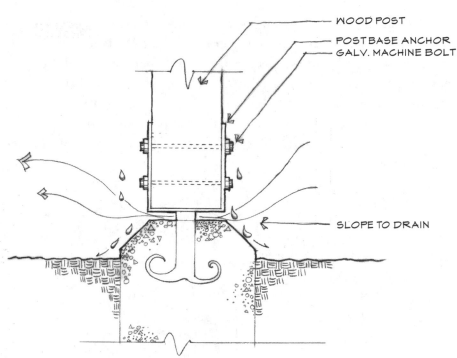

WOOD POST
POST BASE ANCHOR
GALV. MACHINE BOLT

SLOPE TO DRAIN

Figure 3.13 Post footing detail. Edges are rounded or chamfered (angled) to shed water. The raised post anchor prevents moisture buildup and facilitates air circulation. *Source:* Illustration by Jody Estes.

The footing width is sized for the post and should be wide enough so that the anchor will not crack the footing; 3 to 5 in. beyond the anchor is adequate. The depth of the footing should extend at least 2 in. below frost level. The depth also accommodates resistance to the forces of wind, weight, and any other anticipated impacts. The footing should rest on compacted bearing soil. If the soil is organic or unstable, the footing may have to be deeper or some soil may have to be removed and granular fill set below the footing. If the fence is mounted on a continuous footing or masonry wall, the post anchors are preset into the footing or wall cap and the posts bolted to the anchor (see Figure 3.14).

Figure 3.14 Fence atop a masonry wall at the Brooklyn Botanical Garden, on post brackets that are set between the capstones and grouted in place. The bottoms of the vertical boards are set 2 to 3 in. above the top of the wall, allowing for drainage and air circulation.

If a thicker post is desired, a "boxed" outpost or column can be created. A boxed post is built from 1× or greater material, blocked out from the central solid structural wood or steel member (see Figure 3.15). A boxed post has some advantages over a solid member of the same size. Its lighter weight requires a smaller footing, it uses fewer and less costly materials, and the inner structural member has air circulation and protection from weathering. In addition, a boxed post presents an opportunity to create details through the use of moldings.

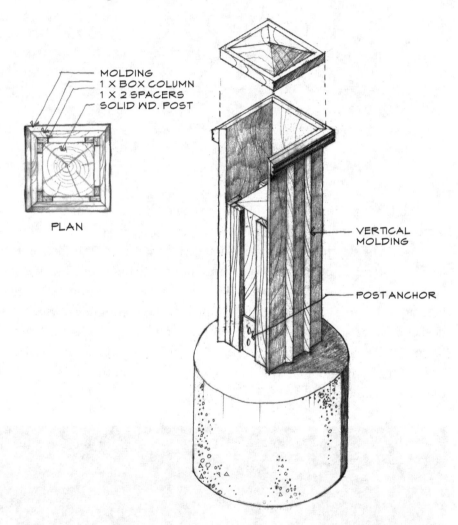

MOLDING
1 X BOX COLUMN
1 X 2 SPACERS
SOLID WD. POST

PLAN

VERTICAL MOLDING

POST ANCHOR

Figure 3.15   In boxed post construction a structural post is anchored to the footing with a post anchor, spacers are fastened to the post, and cladding is attached to the spacers. This method protects the structural post from exposure and provides air circulation. The box can be detailed using wood moldings. Should the box fail, it can be easily replaced, and the structural post remains undamaged. *Source:* Illustration by Jody Estes.

POST CAPS AND FINIALS

The exposed end grain of a fence post is susceptible to rotting. Fence caps are often used to shed water away from the top of the post. Fence caps are typically made of redwood, cedar, cypress, mahogany, or treated wood, although metals, particularly copper, are also used. The cap should extend beyond the face of the post and be either pitched or sloped on all sides to facilitate the shedding of water. A drip groove saw cut on the underside of the cap, between the face of the cap and the face of the post, will prevent water from migrating around the edge of the cap and into the end grain of the post (see Figure 3.16).

The addition of ventilation holes on the bottom side of the cap and at the base of the box post, or in the middle of the post, will help stimulate air circulation in the interior of the box around the structural column (see Figure 3.17, page 56). In addition to the cap, other elements are often added to the design to create a period style, to match existing details on the project, and to prevent migration of water into the post. These elements can include beds, fascias and soffits, crown molding, and plinth blocks for the finial or post (see Figure 3.18).If the box post fails, it can be replaced before the structural column has been compromised.

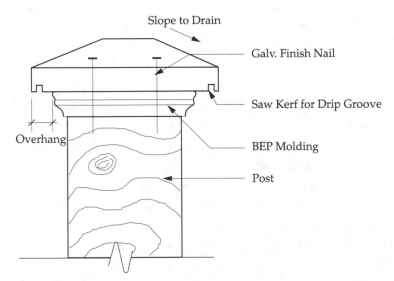

Figure 3.16   Post cap detail. A modest overhang and sawn "kerf" (cut the width of the blade) to prevent water from migrating into the post end grain and cap interface. *Source:* Illustration by Chad Wichers.

Figure 3.18   Built-up post with top cap, base molding, and lower dentils. All pickets and sandwich rails are designed to shed water.

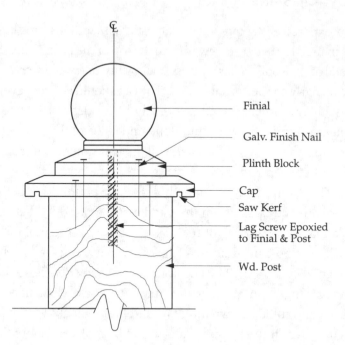

Figure 3.19   Turned balusters, column, rails, and finial create an elegant and solid fence. Note that the dowels, visible at the rail joints in the column, extend through the tenons of the rails and secure them to the post. These forms were originally designed to mimic those made of stone, but were cheaper to build.

Figure 3.20   Assembly including finial, plinth block, and post cap is nailed and screwed into a column, creating a structural composition that is aesthetically pleasing and prevents moisture from penetrating the end grain. *Source:* Illustration by Chad Wichers.

The use of finials has a distinct history. Many styles dictate particular forms of finials; for example, the form of the urn was popular in the Federal period (see Figure 3.8, page 66). The finial is carved, or more commonly turned on a lathe, from either a solid block of wood or a laminated block of clear softwood such as cedar or a hardwood such as mahogony. The finial may be connected to the cap or to an intermediate piece of wood, a block. The finial is attached with a lag bolt epoxied into the finial and screwed into the cap, or it is doweled and glued to the block or post cap. See Figures 3.19 and 3.20.

HORIZONTAL RAILS (STRINGERS)

The horizontal rails stabilize the posts against lateral movement and provide a structural frame for attaching vertical balusters, pickets, boards, or lattice panels. See Figures 3.21 A and B.

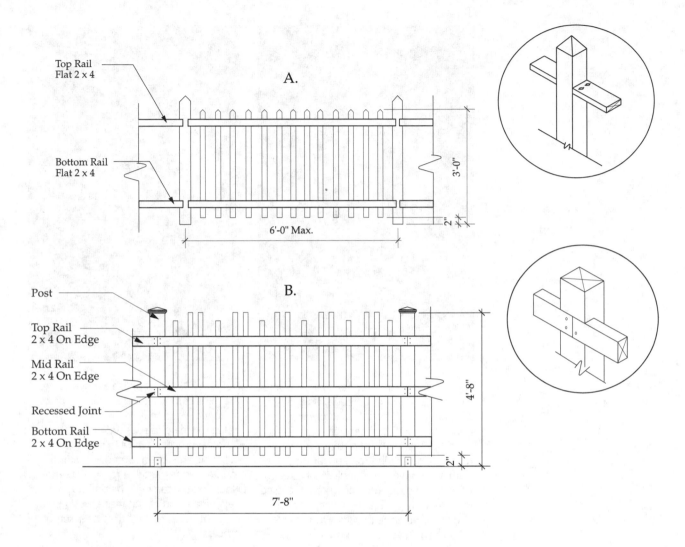

Figures 3.21 A and B (A) Typical two-rail fence panel used for fences up to 4 ft in height. (B) A three-rail fence panel useful for fences up to 8 ft in height. *Source:* Illustration by Chad Wichers.

The number of rails used depends on the height of the fence, style of design, and span of the rails. Except for a single-rail fence (often referred to as a kick rail or guard rail), a minimum of two rails, top and bottom, are required. At heights above 4 ft, or if the vertical boards are narrow in proportion to the height, a third, or middle, rail can be added, providing additional attachment points to prevent cupping or twisting.

The depth for nailing can be increased by setting 2 × 4 rails flat, but spans should not exceed 6 ft and may have to be less with a flat rail, depend-

Figure 3.22   Sandwich rail system, using two parallel rails set on edge, is capable of spanning 8 ft lengths and greater, depending on the dimension of the rails. In addition to their strength, sandwich rails provide an identical appearance on both sides, whereas a single rail has a front and a back. The railings are recessed into the column creating a very strong structure. Note the rail block at the column providing extra support.

Figure 3.23   To establish a fence curve, the rail is composed of several thin pieces of ripped wood that are bent and laminated to create the desired radius. A similar process is used to create the cap rail, which has been routed, providing rounded edges suitable for hand contact. Note that the top rail is beginning to delaminate, indicating that a wet glue may not have been used in the assembly process.

ing on the weight of the material. If the span is 6 ft. or greater, and the weight of the boards considerable, the rails can be set on edge, providing a greater span capability. Often a "sandwich" rail is employed. This form can use thinner material, because there are two members. It also provides a pleasant visual appearance on both sides, as compared with a single rail that often has front and back faces (see Figure 3.22). To create a curved rail, thin pieces of wood material, ¼ to ⅜ in., are bent, often with the use of steam, and glued to the desired radius. Once cured, the curve is set. A curved rail can also be glued and mechanically fastened on-site (see Figure 3.23). To generate less waste, the design should, if possible, be dimensioned to standard lumber lengths. As a rule of thumb, 2 × 4 rails on edge work for lengths up to 8 ft. If the post layout is greater than 8 ft, 2 × 6 or 4 × 4 rails should be employed, depending on the weight of the infill material.

The connection between the rail and post can be detailed in two primary ways, either with a recessed connection or with a mechanical connection. An advantage of recessed connections, lap joints, dados, or mortise and tenons, where the posts are sculpted to receive the rail, is that the weight of one-half of the span of material between posts is transferred to and supported by each of the posts (see Figures 3.24, 3.25, and 3.26). When mechanical connectors such as fence brackets are employed, some of the weight of the rails and boards are transferred to the posts, but significant forces, now actually shear forces, are carried by the connector. This system, although widely used, tends to negate the purpose of the post by relying on the fastener. Potential points of failure are created, in either type of connection, where penetration of the body of the post extends deeper than the layer of preservative treatment. These recessed joints and any prebored holes should receive an application of preservative after they are cut and before the rail is attached.

Figure 3.24 Drilled mortise before treatment in a rusticated fence post, used in the Central Park Restoration project.

Figure 3.25 Carved tenon before treatment on a rusticated fence rail, used in the Central Park Restoration project.

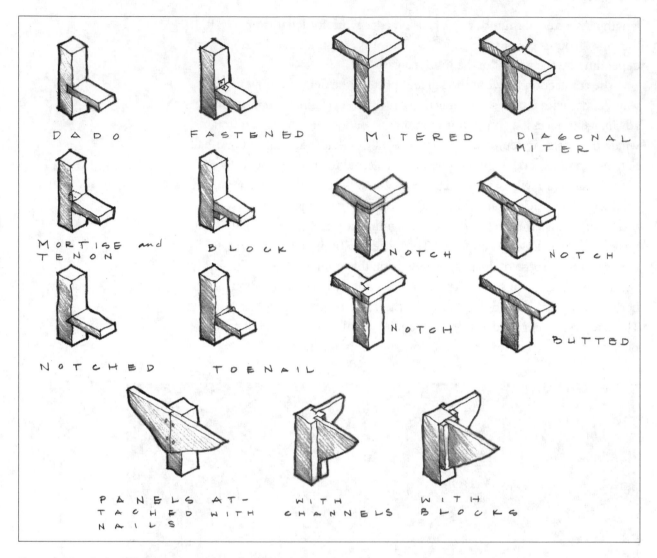

Figure 3.26   Series of joints often used in designing fence rails and caps. *Source:* Illustration by Jody Estes.

PICKETS, BALUSTERS, AND BOARDS

Many fences have vertical elements often referred to as infill, standing in a plane between the posts. The most common infill members are pickets, typically 1 × 2s, 1 × 4s, or 2 × 2s. The usual attachment to the rails is with galvanized nails or screws. Highly crafted fences may have pickets doweled through the rails (see Figure 3.8, page 66). The top ends of the boards or dowels may be cut to drain or shaped to create ornamental features (see

Figure 3.27 Changing the width of the vertical boards and scroll cutting the tops into various "flat finials" transforms the ordinary into a memorable fence.

Figure 3.27). The infill can be designed as a prefabricated system in which the pickets and rails are preassembled as a panel and then inserted into the posts. This is an effective production process if the post spacing is consistent.

Balusters are vertical members set between the top and bottom rails. They range in height and thickness and are in some cases, especially by historic precedent, very elaborate turned pieces (see Figure 3.19, page 74). For the attachment of simple balusters, such as 2 × 2s, a channel can be routed into the top rail to receive the balusters, and the bottoms can be set on a pitched bottom rail or rail cap and mechanically fastened. Other methods include boring or carving recesses into the rails to receive the balusters, or attaching a pair of horizontal members under the top rail to sandwich the top end of the ballusters. The latter method is not recommended on the lower rails, as it will trap water.

Boards can be effectively used on smaller fences (see Figure 3.14, page 71), but their width is maximized frequently in taller fences intended for privacy. The simplest, most solid board fences, using 1 × 4 or 1 × 6 vertical boards placed side to side and mechanically attached to the rails, are the least expensive and often the least interesting. To add visual interest, the edges of the boards are sometimes cut to create a row or field of voids in shapes such as diamonds. In the louvered style, 2 × 4 or 2 × 6 vertical boards are set into angles slotted into the top and bottom rails. This alignment allows visibility from an oblique angle and provides air circulation while offering a large degree of privacy. Other common configurations include the shadow box and the board and batten fences.

The ornamental potential of infills is unlimited; some can be elaborate (as in Figure 3.27) in which each fence element is shaped and crafted. Some can be elegant and simple (as in Figure 3.14, page 71) in which the top ends are cut at differing heights to create an arched panel between the posts. An infill can be chosen to replicate a historic style, to complement the style of an existing building, or to make a personal expression. Beyond style, good design requires that all elements relate to one another aesthetically and functionally.

The post and rail fence, of which there are many variations, is the simplest and probably the oldest of fence designs. The form derives from the zigzag, or Virginia rail fence, in which the rails were stacked atop each other in a zigzag pattern around a post, or with the post eliminated altogether. The style was utilitarian for corralling animals but consumed a great quantity of material to build. The post and rail in its simplest form is a wood post connected by two or more horizontal rails. A rustic variation is the split rail fence, using rails, typically split from a log, with a minimum of shaping at the ends. The rail ends are inserted into prebored holes in the post, sometimes bypassing each other with an overlapping of the horizontal members.

Figure 3.28   One of the oldest fence styles and still in use today, the split rail or post and rail fence. Historically, the fence posts were bored with mortises and the rails passed through the posts. *Source:* Illustration by Jody Estes.

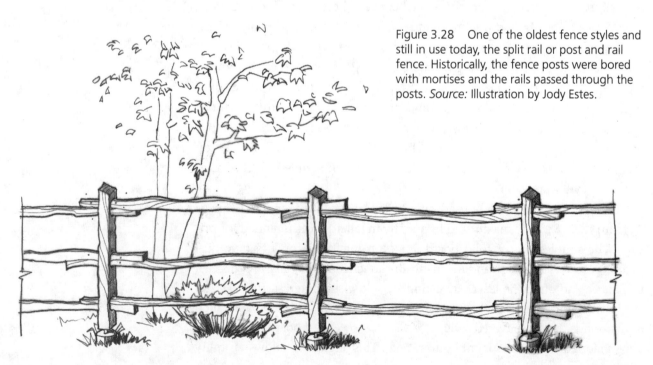

Figure 3.29 A hybrid of the post and rail with an elaborately turned post. The machine-cut rails are set into, rather than passed through, the posts.

Figure 3.30 The basket weave style of fence is visually impenetrable. Thin horizontal boards are woven between intermediate vertical members.

The post and rail remains popular in rural areas, and highly ornamented examples can be found in New England and in the Southern states. Because this fence contains no vertical members other than the posts, it provides little resistance to wind loads. Such fences are considered "transparent fences" because they provide very little privacy, but by adding climbing vines, visual screening can be increased. The rambling and wild roses on a split rail fence are a New England seaside vernacular. Transparency and security, if desired, can be achieved by using wire mesh attached to the posts and rails (see Figures 3.29 and 3.31 C).

Solid, slatted, and picket fences are, in principle, an extension of the post and rail, adding vertical members that increase the density and visual privacy of the fencing (see Figures 3.31 A–C). Maximizing density are the solid fences, including vertical tongue and groove or shiplapped boards, solid panels, shadow box fences in which the boards alternate on each side of the rails, and board and batten fences (see Figures 3.30 and 3.32 A–C).

RELATED SPECIFICATIONS
03200—Concrete Reinforcement
03250—Concrete Accessories
03300—Cast-in-Place Concrete
06050—Fasteners and Adhesives
06100—Rough Carpentry
06200—Finish Carpentry
06300—Preservation Treatment
06400—Architectural Woodwork
09900—Painting

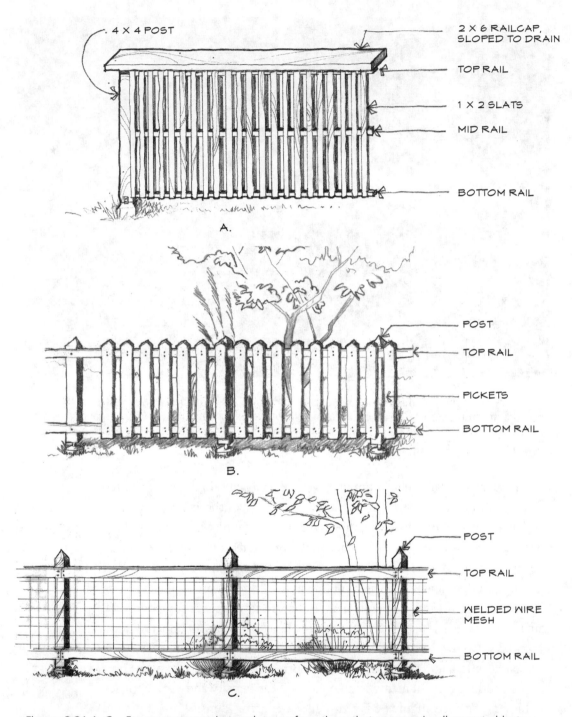

4 X 4 POST

2 X 6 RAILCAP, SLOPED TO DRAIN

TOP RAIL

1 X 2 SLATS

MID RAIL

BOTTOM RAIL

A.

POST

TOP RAIL

PICKETS

BOTTOM RAIL

B.

POST

TOP RAIL

WELDED WIRE MESH

BOTTOM RAIL

C.

Figures 3.31 A–C   Fences can range in translucency from those that are very visually penetrable, to those that are more screenlike, as illustrated in (C). (A) The narrow width and spacing of vertical members allows slight visual penetration. (B) The classic picket fence can create a high proportion of visual openness by increasing the distance between the pickets. (C) Virtually transparent, the wire mesh screen fence used to restrict physical access is not intended for visual privacy. *Source:* Illustration by Jody Estes.

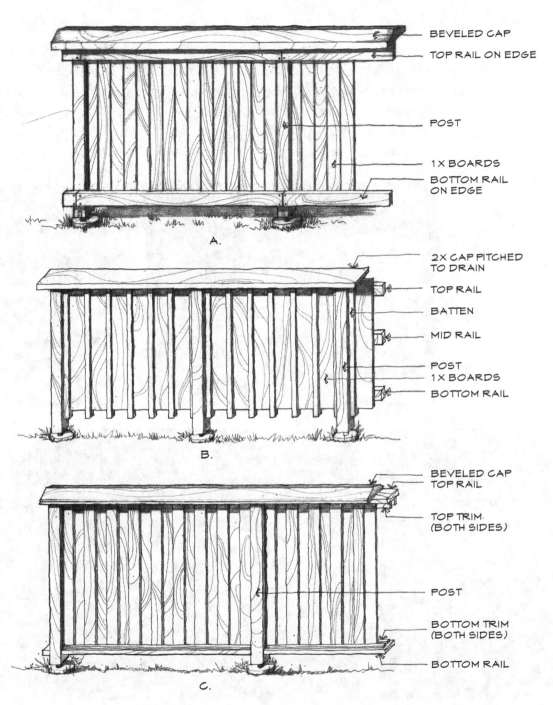

Figures 3.32 A–C   Solid board fences are common when privacy is desired and visual access restricted. (A) Solid board fence with rails on end is one of the most common and least costly types of solid board varieties. (B) In the board and batten 1 × 2 pieces are placed on the vertical joints between the boards. (C) In the shadow box the boards are offset front and back between the rails, allowing a slight visual penetration and air circulation between the boards. The boards must be 2× if the midrail is eliminated. *Source:* Illustration by Jody Estes.

A second type includes semitransparent fences, in which voids are spaced with varying degrees of visual penetration, employing wood screens, lattice, pickets, and balustrades (see Figure 3.33). The design variation within this type is very broad, and solid, semitransparent, and transparent approaches can be combined in the same design with different infills above and below midrail. Overhead trellising, cantilevering from the posts, can also be incorporated in fence design. See Figures 3.34 through 3.39.

Figure 3.33   A horizontal rail fence abuts a vertical picket fence and illustrates the increase in opaqueness and formality, as one moves from the rail fence to the picket fence.

Figure 3.34   As an alternative to rails or pickets, a diagonal stick-work pattern creates an openness and rhythm not commonly seen. Note that the bottom rail is set on top of a raised wood beam, creating a wood curb.

Figure 3.35   A pattern similar to that found in Figure 3.34, but through the choice of material, unmilled wood, an informal character is achieved.

Figure 3.36 This method of using turned balusters to penetrate a double-pitched top rail creates an exceptionally strong fence. In constructing the fence, very few fasteners are needed, and when built properly, this design provides great durability. The holes must be rebored if replacement of the balusters is required.

Figure 3.37A An unusual curved sandwich rail transition with mitered corners. Note the flashing on the far "structural" rail versus the near face rail. The rail top should be pitched away from the balustrades to provide good drainage and air circulation.

Figure 3.37B Water can infiltrate where fasteners are attached and at the joints between wood members. In this example the joints in the rail cap and the post and rail connection are showing signs of deterioration.

Figure 3.38 This scroll-work bracketed corner provides an ornamental transition in the elevation change from rail cap to post extension.

GATES

A gate is the focal point within a fence or masonry wall and can occasionally be found as a stand-alone element in the landscape. When used with a fence, it can be designed as either a complementing or contrasting element. Because a gate is a movable structural component, it is critical that it be designed to counter the forces to which it is subjected. Gateposts are typically oversized to bear the stresses caused by the weight and motion of the gate. Depending on the dimensions of the gate, 6×6 in. solid wood post members, or steel I beams with wood built-up box post surrounds are often used (see Figures 3.39 and 3.40). A post should be deeply embedded or mounted on an over-sized footing to withstand the pull of the gate. A 3 ft depth for a small gate, and a depth of at least 4 ft for a tall or wide gate, is recommended regardless of frost depth. For large gates at entry drives or very wide pedestrian paths, a structural engineer should be consulted to size the bearing posts and attachment mechanisms.

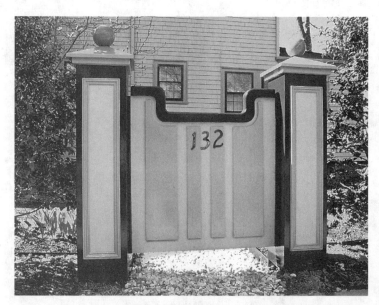

Figure 3.39   An oversized box post, finials, paint, and a raised paneled gate create a visual focal point, marking the entry to the site.

Figure 3.40   This simple board fence is constructed without a box frame, relying on the horizontal rails and hidden brace behind for stability.

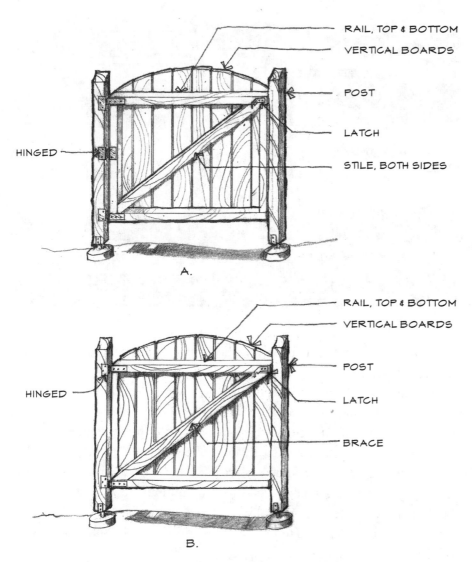

RAIL, TOP & BOTTOM

VERTICAL BOARDS

POST

LATCH

STILE, BOTH SIDES

HINGED

A.

RAIL, TOP & BOTTOM

VERTICAL BOARDS

POST

LATCH

BRACE

HINGED

B.

Figures 3.41 A and B   Two primary framing methods are employed in gate construction. (A) The box frame, *above,* and (B) "Z" frame, *below,* both have horizontal rails, but the box frame has two vertical members (stiles) on each side, allowing a third midhinge to be used. The box frame also allows joinery, particularly lap joints, between stile and rail. *Source:* Illustration by Jody Estes.

There are two basic gate frames, the Z-frame and the box frame (see Figures 3.41 A and B). The Z-frame is simpler and is best used for gates of 3 ft or less in width. It tends to be less formal than the box frame, and the rails and brace can be set flat, creating a thinner profile, whereas in the box style the frame must be set on edge (see Figure 3.42).

The Z-frame is composed of a top and a bottom rail joined by a diagonal brace crossing from the hinge-side bottom to the latch-side top. The hinges are attached to the top and bottom rails, and because the Z-frame has no vertical side members (stiles), the use of a middle hinge is not possible (see Figure 3.40).

Figure 3.42 A box frame gate carries the horizontal lines of the post and rail fence through the frame. The post on the left both receives the gate to the right and supports the gate to the left. The pedestrian gate *(right)*, is hung on "T" hinges, and the gate to the left is hung on ball and pinion hinges, often used for heavier swing gates.

Like a frame for a panel door, the box frame gate is composed of vertical members (stiles) and horizontal members (rails). For this type of gate, two stiles, one on each side, and a minimum of two rails, top and bottom, are employed, allowing the use of a top, bottom, and middle hinge. A middle rail can be used to support pickets, boards, or panels, or for structural stability if the gate is tall. The stiles are usually built of 2 × 4s; 2 × 6s may be used for tall gates. The rails, depending on design, often have a larger bottom rail, 2 × 6 or 2 × 8, and a smaller 2 × 4 top and midrail; however, these should be designed to relate proportionally.

There are several ways to join the rails and stiles. The simplest is to nail or screw the pieces together. To increase stability and longevity, a variety of joints are used to attach a stile to a rail, including mortise and tenons, doweled joints, lap joints, and wood "biscuits." The mortise and tenon is the strongest of the joints and, when crafted well, can be bonded with an adhesive, thus avoiding the need for mechanical fasteners altogether. The doweled joint uses wooden pegs and glue to join the rail and the stile together, avoiding the penetration of the wood surface with mechanical fasteners. The lap joint is easy to fabricate, provides a large area for gluing, and with a strong waterproof glue can be clamped and jointed without fasteners.

If the intended purpose is visual effect more than security, the gate should be designed to be as light as possible, minimizing the forces on the post. A common problem in gates is the tendency to rack or sag. To resist this inclination, gates are designed with bracing. The design can reveal the 2 × 4 or 1 × 4 bracing pattern with either a diagonal, Z, or X configuration. The result is a semitransparent gate. To create a solid privacy screen, the bracing is used as a nailer upon which the pickets or boards are secured, increasing the weight of the gate. If the diagonal line created by the bracing is not desired, a galvanized turnbuckle and rod can be used in lieu of wood, which can be sandwiched or hidden by pickets to minimize the visibility of the brace (see Figures 3.43 A–D).

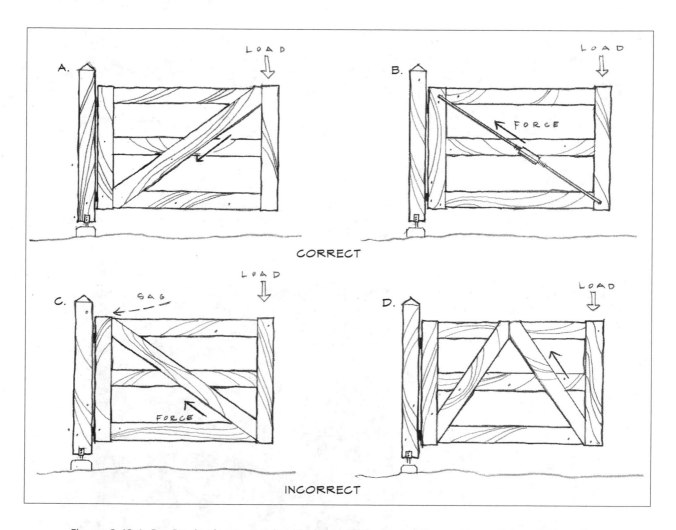

Figures 3.43 A–D   Bracing in any gate is critical to resist the loads falling on the nonhinged side and the forces put on the upper hinge side. Thus, a brace that directs the force to the lower hinge is the recommended option (A). Although not the best, the tie rod with a toggle bolt (B) that allows for adjustment is better than placing additional pressure on the upper hinge by improperly placing the brace (C and D). *Source:* Illustration by Jody Estes.

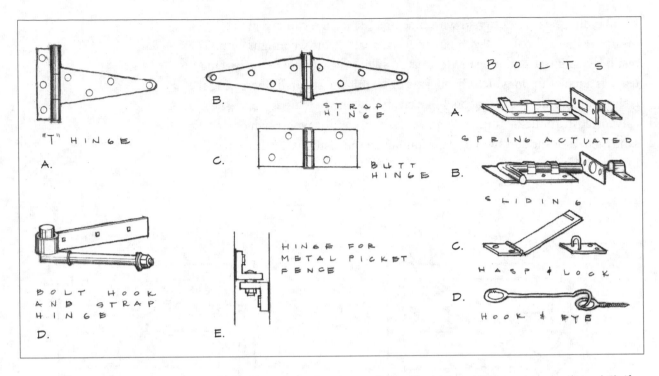

Figure 3.44   A variety of hinges and bolt-locking mechanisms are available. The butt and "T" are common (A and C); if the gate is heavy the ball and pinion should be considered (D and E). The bolt mechanisms range from the simplest (D) to the most secure (A). *Source:* Illustration by Jody Estes.

Figure 3.45   A simple wrought iron latch provides an ornamental feature on this sandwich framed gate. Note the cap rail angle cut to accommodate the swing of the gate.

The post must be plumb and in line for the gate to swing and close easily. As a rule of thumb, assume ¼ in. clearance on the hinge side and ⅜ in. on the latch side if the frame is 1½ in. thick. If it is greater, add ⅝ in. on the latch side. For taller gates, ½ in. on each side allows for expansion and ease of swing.

The gate connection from the swing side stile to the post where the hinge is mounted is a critical one, and the hardware designed for hanging includes butt, T, strap, and strap hinge/bolt systems (see Figures 3.44 and 3.45). Each system offers varying degrees of strength, and each requires a different amount of surface area for attachment.

A 3 to 4 in. butt hinge, with the leaves of the hinge mortised into the post and the frame, is usually adequate for small gates. A surface-mounted T hinge is recommended for larger gates. Strap hinges should be employed on gates exceeding 5 ft in width, as in a driveway entry gate when the gate is flush mounted to the posts. A strap and bolt hinge allows for easy detachment of the gate when removal is regularly required. Each of these options offers a different level of security and rigidity.

For securing heavy gates with the potential to sag, a pintle-type hinge may provide the proper support. The pintle, or male half, is an **L**-shaped steel pin screwed into the post. A corresponding female half, the eye, is bolted top and bottom to the gate rail or stile, and the eyes are set onto the pins. This system allows for easy removal of the gate to facilitate maintenance and can carry substantial weights, depending on the gauge of the pintle.

The second piece of hardware used in gate fabrication is a locking mechanism. Options range from the simplest hook and eye to spring-activated bolts. Other mechanisms include sliding bolts, hasp and locking hackle, and thumb hatches (see Figures 3.44, 3.45, and 3.46 A–C).

The hasp mechanism is designed to receive a lock; others secure the gate without locking. A stop on the latch post will prevent the gate from swinging past the post and stressing the hinge. The stop can be as simple as a strip of board attached to the post. A spring can be attached to the gate and connected to the post, creating a constant tension and keeping the gate in the closed position when unbolted. See Figures 3.46 A–C and 3.47 A–C.

All hardware required to hang and operate the gate should be considered for structural stability, aesthetics, and corrosion resistance. All hardware should be galvanized or stainless steel (see Figure 3.48).

RELATED SPECIFICATIONS

03200 — Concrete Reinforcement
03250 — Concrete Accessories
03300 — Cast-in-Place Concrete
06050 — Fasteners and Adhesives
06200 — Finish Carpentry

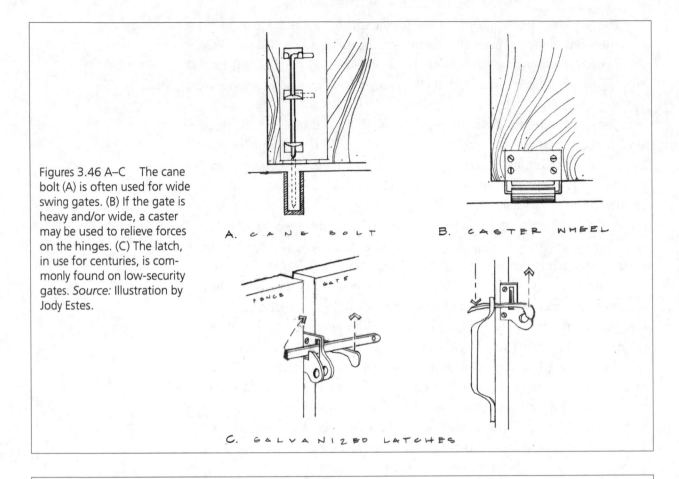

Figures 3.46 A–C   The cane bolt (A) is often used for wide swing gates. (B) If the gate is heavy and/or wide, a caster may be used to relieve forces on the hinges. (C) The latch, in use for centuries, is commonly found on low-security gates. *Source:* Illustration by Jody Estes.

A. CANE BOLT

B. CASTER WHEEL

C. GALVANIZED LATCHES

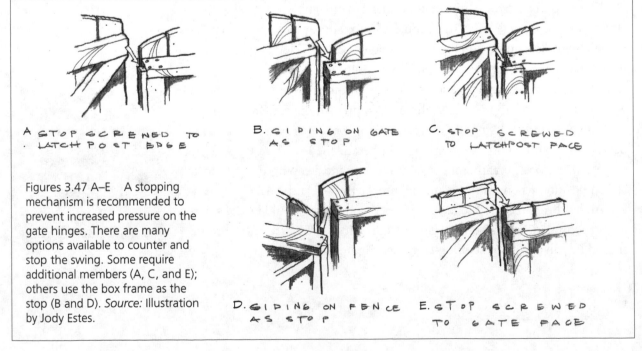

A STOP SCREWED TO LATCHPOST EDGE

B. GIDING ON GATE AS STOP

C. STOP SCREWED TO LATCHPOST FACE

Figures 3.47 A–E   A stopping mechanism is recommended to prevent increased pressure on the gate hinges. There are many options available to counter and stop the swing. Some require additional members (A, C, and E); others use the box frame as the stop (B and D). *Source:* Illustration by Jody Estes.

D. GIDING ON FENCE AS STOP

E. STOP SCREWED TO GATE FACE

Figure 3.48   Adding two countercurves to a simple box frame gate provides an extended hinge side stile to accommodate a top hinge placed high on the post.

RETAINING WALLS

Although wood is not often used to construct freestanding walls, the use of wood timber for retaining wall construction is quite common, particularly in residential and small commercial projects. The use of timbers for retaining can be traced back to the early days when logs were used to build wood cribbing structures that retained soils for bridge abutments and to stabilize railroad beds. Similar structures built in logging camps were called skidders and were used to slide fallen logs onto transport trucks. Their remnants can still be found on old logging roads in New England, and even today lumber bridge abutments and railroad trestle constructions can be found in the rural parts of the country.

In the interim, from log crib walls to treated timber retaining walls, milled timbers treated with creosote preservative were used. Today, the use of creosote as a preservative is restricted and instead pressure-treated 6 × 6 or

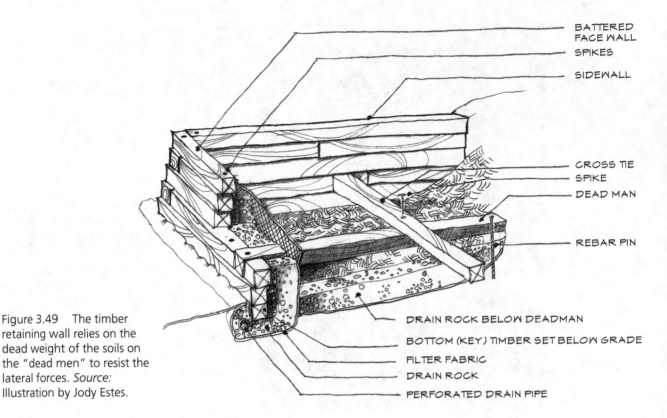

BATTERED
FACE WALL

SPIKES

SIDEWALL

CROSS TIE

SPIKE

DEAD MAN

REBAR PIN

DRAIN ROCK BELOW DEADMAN

BOTTOM (KEY) TIMBER SET BELOW GRADE

FILTER FABRIC

DRAIN ROCK

PERFORATED DRAIN PIPE

Figure 3.49   The timber retaining wall relies on the dead weight of the soils on the "dead men" to resist the lateral forces. *Source:* Illustration by Jody Estes.

8×8 timbers, rated for ground contact, are more commonly used. The choice of 6×6s or 8×8s is one of aesthetics, cost, and availability of timbers.

There are two concerns in designing a timber retaining wall. First, the amount of resistance designed into the wall is derived from the weight of the soil being retained. The vertical timber wall is tied back into the soil bank with timber tiebacks, or "dead men," to resist the force exerted by the back-fill. Second, when wet soil freezes, it expands, exerting increased pressure on the wall; therefore, drainage through the wall is critical (see Figure 3.49).

DRAINAGE

To facilitate drainage and create a level plane for the first course of the timbers, a trench is excavated following the alignment of the wall. The depth is equal to one timber, 6 in. if a 6×6 is used, with an additional 6 to 8 in. for drain rock, for a total of 12 to 14 in. A sheet of filter fabric is laid the length of the trench, with extra fabric equal to the height of the wall at the back and with a few feet at the front. This trench will hold a layer of drain gravel, providing a level pad and allowing movement of water under the wall and into a perforated drainpipe placed below and in front of the bottom timber (see Figures 3.49 and 3.50 A–D).

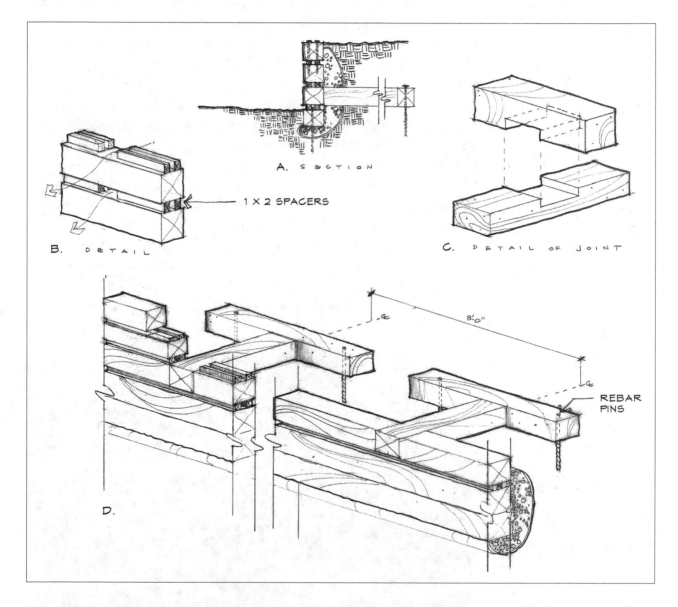

Figures 3.50 A–D The wall timbers are pinned to the subgrade and spiked together (A). The dead men are interlocked into the wall and at the point farthest from the wall they are pinned into the subgrade (D). The tail should be jointed into the tie as shown in (C). By using spacers in the vertical wall, voids are created, allowing water to pass through, relieving the hydrostatic pressure, and revealing a shadow line (B). *Source:* Illustration by Jody Estes.

SETTING THE TIMBERS

The first and bottom timber is placed and leveled on the gravel and should be flush or slightly below finish grade at the toe of the wall. After two courses of timbers are laid, tieback timbers are placed perpendicularly atop the wall timber with the front face end grain set slightly back to accommodate the batter. The batter is the angle of the wall face, and it increases the resistance to the soil pressure. Common batters are designated as 1.12 (or 1.8), meaning that for every vertical rise of 12 (8) in., the wall slopes to back to the soil 1 in. (see Figure 3.49). The tieback should extend as far as is reasonable; a rule of thumb is that the length of the tieback should extend back into the soil no less than the height of the wall. However, this also depends on the slope of the bank being retained and on the height of the wall (because any wall more than 5 ft in height should be designed by a structural engineer).

A trench of gravel should be laid below the tiebacks, which are predrilled and attached to the wall with 12 in. galvanized spikes, oversized nails (see Figure 3.49). The opposite end to be backfilled is predrilled, and a ⅝ × 24 in. piece of reinforcing bar is driven through, pinning the tieback to the bank. A cross tie timber placed parallel with the front wall and following the end of the tiebacks connects the sidewalls and the tiebacks (see Figures 3.50 and 3.51). The front and sidewalls can then be stacked to the desired height, and

Figure 3.51 Spacers between the timbers form a shadow line, adding visual interest to the wall face.

Figure 3.52   Timber walls can be used to form extensive, cost-effective terraces on sloping grades.

if desired, additional tiebacks and cross ties can be placed; however, the lower the tiebacks, the greater the soil weight, which maximizes the wall's resistance (see Figure 3.52). As the wall is being backfilled, gravel is laid at a thickness of 12 in. behind the wall and wrapped with the extra filter fabric. This vertical wall of gravel will intercept any migrating water and channel it to the base of the wall. A perforated drain pipe laid below the timbers will convey the collected water away from the structure.

If the wall is to be used as a seating wall, 2 × 8s or 2 × 10s can be edge routed and used to cap the wall for comfort.

RELATED SPECIFICATIONS
06050 — Fasteners and
            Adhesives
06100 — Rough
            Carpentry

FREESTANDING WALLS

The use of wood or timbers for freestanding walls is not very common. Timbers placed horizontally into the flanges of steel I-beam vertical columns were popular as sound barriers for a period of time, but have largely been replaced by precast concrete structures.

Two factors account for the preference of other materials over wood in freestanding wall construction. First is the lack of durability. Masonry materials, although generally more expensive, provide a longer service life and reduced maintenance, as compared with wood. Second, the cost of materials, particularly if the wood members are placed vertically, can be high, and when the prevalence of degradation below grade is considered, most designers opt for some form of masonry monolithic or unit product.

The consideration that accounts for the few examples of vertical wood walls is aesthetics. As seen in Figure 3.53 A, the short wall in the Brooklyn Botanical Garden is reflective of the other materials used in the garden and makes reference to the traditional bamboo retaining walls popular in some of the historic gardens. The use of a similar style in a children's playground (see Figure 3.53 B) responds to the form of a curved freestanding wall that can be achieved when the members are used vertically, but would be difficult to achieve if the members were placed horizontally.

Figure 3.53 B   In this play area on the campus of Louisiana State University the vertical 6 × 6s are used to define the space and provide the children with climbing opportunities.

Figure 3.53 A   Rounded vertical pressure-treated timbers form an elegant retaining wall at the Brooklyn Botanical Japanese Garden.

In this case, the material was chosen primarily for safety, as the wood members provide a more forgiving surface than a similar wall of masonry would. Thus, if contact is made, a child will suffer less injury.

DECKS

The prevalence of wood decks attached to, or independent of, a house is a relatively recent phenomenon in Western cultures. Because wood was used for many other purposes—fuel, railroad and bridge construction—paved patios, dirt yards, and formal lawns were common for gathering areas and wood was limited to house or fence construction. The closest forerunner of the deck may be the expansive porches found in the Southern or Florida style of housing. Variations of the type can be found in the screen porches of New England, in the verandahs of the grand antebellum mansions of the South, and in the expansive roofed front porches of plantation style houses found in the southeastern Gulf States and the Caribbean. The historic use of decks in China and Japan can be traced back hundreds of years. In the Chinese garden a miniature representation of nature with symbolic lakes, mountains, and trees is viewed from an open wood-decked pavilion. In Japan the deck became an extension of the pavilion, often appearing to float out over a water body. Wood benches were incorporated into the framing, and the orientation of the deck was directed toward specific views. In Chinese and Japanese cultures the deck often served the individual or family as a platform from which to view the garden or as a place for contemplation. Such use is in contrast to that of Western cultures, in which the deck is a focal point for entertaining and socializing, its size sometimes overwhelming what remains of the garden. In suburban areas, where space is plentiful, decks have evolved into a rambling style, less formal than their prototypical urban porch or verandah. Decks are also used to link the house to the outdoors on steeply sloped sites, where patios are not possible.

The framing of a deck is similar to the framing of a traditional house, designed as a load-bearing structure. The major difference is that the deck framing must stand rigid without the stability of floor sheathing, continuous foundations, walls, or a roof. A deck is typically built without solid sides or an impermeable covering above, and it is constantly exposed to the weathering effects of the climate—rain, snow, and temperature changes. Prolonged

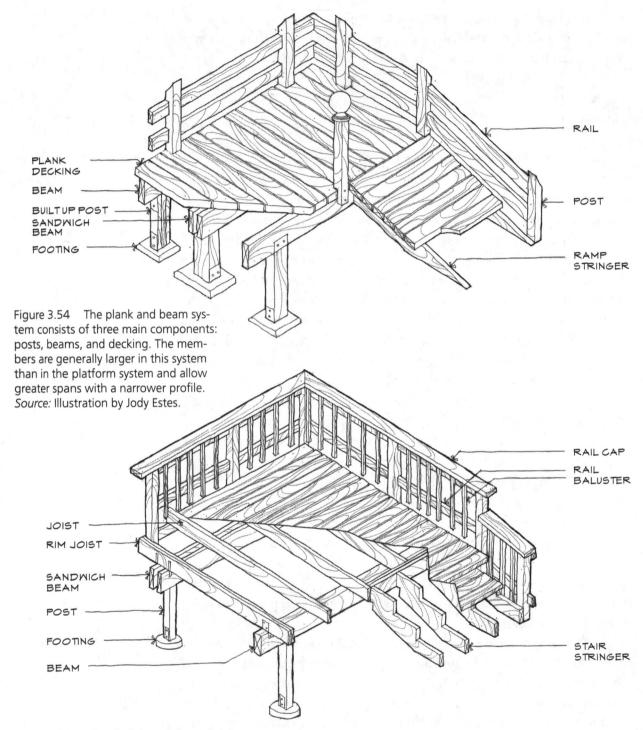

PLANK
DECKING

BEAM

BUILT UP POST

SANDWICH
BEAM

FOOTING

RAIL

POST

RAMP
STRINGER

Figure 3.54   The plank and beam system consists of three main components: posts, beams, and decking. The members are generally larger in this system than in the platform system and allow greater spans with a narrower profile. *Source:* Illustration by Jody Estes.

RAIL CAP

RAIL
BALUSTER

JOIST

RIM JOIST

SANDWICH
BEAM

POST

FOOTING

BEAM

STAIR
STRINGER

Figure 3.55   The platform system uses joists as intermediary members, giving a deeper profile and reduced spans. *Source:* Illustration by Jody Estes.

exposure to moisture promotes the growth of molds and fungi and results in unsafe, slippery surfaces. Safety is also an issue when the deck is raised above finish grade. Accidental falls over the edge are a concern, especially with younger children. Beyond safety, other features—form and integration with other built or natural elements, level changes, site grades, entries, and traffic flow—will influence the design of the structure.

Before designing, all codes, including the Uniform Building Code (UBC) and all local codes applicable to the structure, should be reviewed and adhered to.

SYSTEMS

There are two structural systems commonly employed in deck construction, platform framing and plank-and-beam framing. The difference between the two is relatively simple (see Figures 3.54 and 3.55). Platform framing utilizes an intermediary horizontal structural member, the joist, to transfer loads from the decking to the beam. The joists are typically spaced 16 to 24 in. apart, and because of their size, 2×6 or 2×8, allow for a greater distance between the beams below than in the plank-and-beam system. The thickness of the joists must be included in the finished profile; thus, this system produces a thicker substructure.

Plank-and-beam framing utilizes a single horizontal structural member, a beam, to transfer the loads from the decking to the post. Eliminating the joists allows for a lower profile, but plank-and-beam decking typically spans greater distances and requires a thicker material than that used in the platform method.

BASIC FRAMING MEMBERS: FOOTING, PIER, POST, BEAM, AND JOIST

In designing a structure, the process is thought through in reverse of the actual building process. The spacing of the members is determined by the span of the members above; thus, a top-down sequence makes sense. As described at the beginning of this chapter, the process becomes somewhat circular, as aesthetic decisions may require dimensional changes of the members and the necessary recalculations. The order in this description of decking follows the structure as it is built (see Figure 3.55).

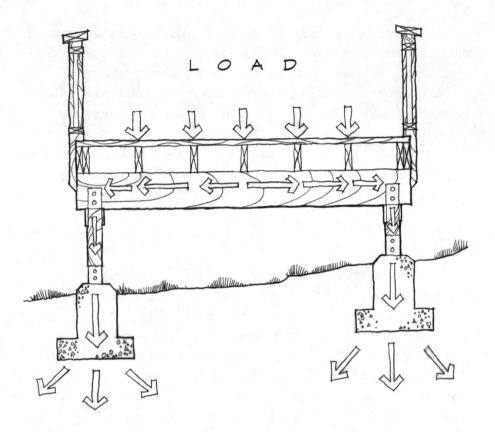

Figure 3.56   The transfer of loads through the decking structure to the joist, the beams to the post, and finally through the footing and into the subgrade. *Source:* Illustration by Jody Estes.

FOUNDATION

The structural integrity of a deck begins with the foundation, and unlike the continuous perimeter concrete foundation of a house, deck foundations are typically footings, which receive concentrated loads at specific isolated points. To create a stable structure, the framing must transfer the loads at the corners to the posts and to intermediate points along the beam's length. The loads that are transferred begin with the live loads (people on the deck), to the decking, and the live loads plus the increasing dead loads are transferred down through the joists, to the beams, and to the posts above grade, and through the concrete pier and spread footing into the ground (see Figures 3.56 and 3.57).

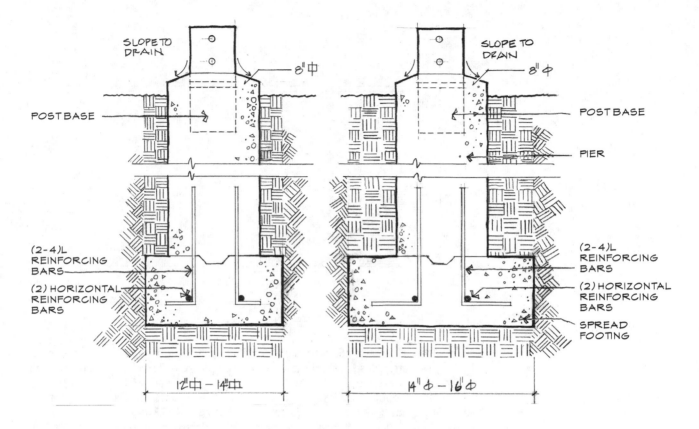

Figure 3.57   The pier footing comprises a concrete spread footing and pier; both are cast in place. The pier can be either round or square. A post anchor or a beam seat is cast into the pier to receive a structural wood member. *Source:* Illustration by Jody Estes.

The footing is sized to carry the total load, which is determined by combining the live and dead loads. If the loads are equally distributed, one can determine the footprint of the footing: Divide the total load on all the footings by the number of footings; then divide the load on each footing by the bearing capacity of the soil (see Figure 3.58).

To determine the total load, multiply the total square footage of the deck by the design live and dead loads. Most codes require a deck to support an estimated live load of 40 lb per sq ft (psf) (people and movable items on the deck), combined with a 10 lb psf dead load (the weight of the deck itself), for a total of 50 psf; however, some require a structurally designed load of 60 psf. Check with the applicable codes for the locale of the project.

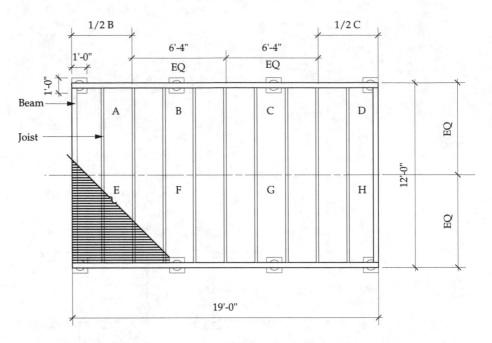

Figure 3.58   Size calculations for a decking footing: The tributary load is the area each footing will carry; thus, in this illustration it is the distance halfway between the footing to the east or west and the distance halfway between the beam to the north or south. Note that the tributary loads carried by the quads A, D, E, and H will be half of those carried by quads B, C, F, or G. In square inches, B is 76 in. × 72 in = 5,472 in. Converted to square feet, 5,472 sq in. divided by 144 sq in. = 38 sq ft. To calculate the pressure, multiply 38 sq ft by 50 lb pressure per sq ft (psf), which equals 1,900 psf. Because the soil bearing capacity is 1,500 psf, the spread must be greater than 12 in. × 12 in. Dividing 1,900 psf by 1,500 psf gives a footing size of 1.26 sq ft, or 1.12 ft × 1.12 ft. Converting to inches and rounding up, the adequate dimensions will be 14 in. × 14 in. *Source:* Illustration by Chad Wichers.

RELATED SPECIFICATIONS

03100 — Concrete Formwork
03200 — Concrete Reinforcement
03250 — Concrete Accessories
03300 — Cast-in-Place Concrete
03370 — Concrete Curing

For estimating purposes, a beam carries the weight of the deck halfway between it and the next beam or ledger, which is called the tributary load. Inorganic soils, those with high contents of sand, gravel, or inorganic silts, have a bearing capacity of 1,500 psf or more (check with the local building department or conservation agent). In this soil condition the bearing capacity for a 12 × 12 in. footing is 1,500 lbs. If the soils contain higher amounts of clay or organic material, the bearing capacity may be less, resulting in a greater footing footprint. The dimensions for concrete footings carrying normal loads in good soils are 12 × 12 in. to 14 × 14 in., and for round footings a diameter of 14 to 16 in. In most situations a 6 in. deep spread footing is adequate, but for heavy loads or for a spread footing greater than 16 in. on a side, the depth will increase to 8 in. The number of footings required is related to the tributary loads that will be carried. For large decks an engineer should be consulted, but these figures provide a general rule of thumb for footing designs.

The footing, typically a poured concrete structure, must sit below the point where soil freezes in winter. Information on the depth of freezing can be acquired from local building departments. Frost heave is a condition of water, temperature, and soil permeability that results when water in the soil freezes and expands. It can lift a footing, resulting in racking or structural failure of a deck. In areas prone to frost heave or with poor drainage, additional drainage material such as drain rock can be placed below the footings to reduce water retention in the soil. For additional strength, a grid of #4 rebar can be embedded into the footing 8 in. on center (oc). See Figure 3.57.

PIERS AND POSTS

The simplest footing is a pier block, a precast battered square concrete block with an embedded post anchor, on which the post is bolted. Unless set below grade, piers will not resist any frost heave, and because of their size, have limits on their load-carrying capacity. Some codes require a more permanent cast-in-place footing (check with local codes).

Concrete piers, required by code in many parts of the country, are not susceptible to insect infestations and are decayproof and very strong. A pier is typically poured on top of a spread footing that has been stubbed out with a minimum of two #4 reinforcing bars if the pier extends more than 6 in. above grade to tie the pier to the footing. The spread footing is a 6 to 8 in. thick square form typically 6 to 8 in. greater in width than the pier diameter. After the spread footing pour has set, a concrete pier form is placed on top of the footing. The form can be constructed of wood to pour a square or rectangular column. Alternately, cylindrical paper forms, "sono" tubes, can be used, which are available in diameter sizes from 4 in., increasing in 2 in. increments up to 18 in., and in diameters of 24 in. and 36 in. See Figures 3.59 A and B.

An 8 in. diameter pier, with two to four L-shaped vertical #4 reinforcing bars embedded in the footing, is usually adequate for a 4 × 4 wood post. A 10 to 12 in. diameter pier is recommended for a 6 × 6 post. After the concrete is poured, a galvanized steel post anchor can be embedded in the top of the form to receive a post or beam. The post anchor separates the end grain of the post from the concrete surface and creates a ½ in. air gap below the post that ensures good ventilation below the end grain of the wood post. The top of the

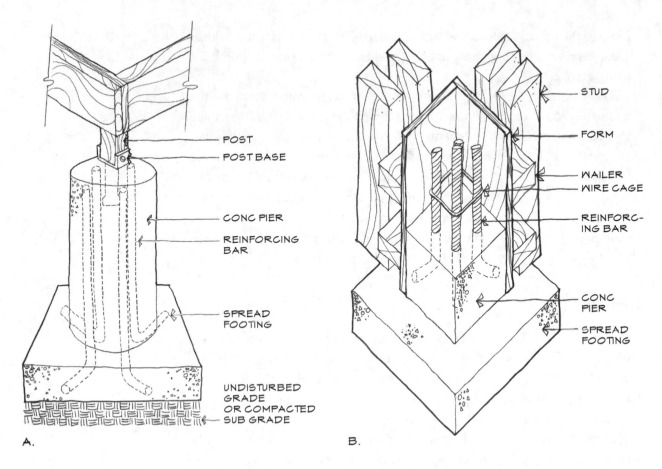

POST
POST BASE

CONC PIER

REINFORCING
BAR

SPREAD
FOOTING

UNDISTURBED
GRADE
OR COMPACTED
SUB GRADE

A.

STUD

FORM

WAILER
WIRE CAGE

REINFORC-
ING BAR

CONC
PIER

SPREAD
FOOTING

B.

Figures 3.59 A and B   The spread footing and pier are connected through L-shaped reinforcing bars. It is common to extend the pier above finish grade before attaching the wood post. The post extends from the beam top of the pier to the base of the beam. *Source:* Illustration by Jody Estes.

concrete pier should be hand-formed to provide an adequate pitch sloping away from the post base, reducing any water buildup that may infiltrate the end grain (see Figure 3.57).

The intermediary wood post transfers the load from the beam and joists to the pier or footing. If the finished elevation of the deck is less than 1 to 2 ft from grade, the concrete piers typically extend above grade to receive the beam, eliminating the wood post. If a wood post is used, a 4 × 4 post is often adequate to transfer the loads; however, many designers specify larger 6 × 6 posts and double notch the posts on either side to provide a 1½ in. seat that will receive a sandwich beam. In this method a 2½ in. tongue is left on the post, which protrudes up through the beam and through which the beam and post can be bolted together (see Figure 3.60)

A post need not be one solid member, especially if it is greater than 8 in. in either dimension. Timbers of this dimension can be expensive or difficult to find. An alternative is to build up a post using standard 2× dimensional lumber. A 6 × 6 post can be fabricated from four pieces of 2 × 6, glued and laminated (see Figure 3.61).

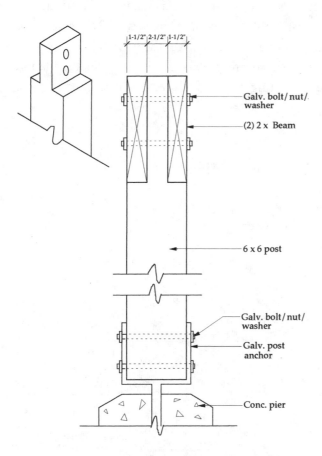

Figure 3.60   The notched beam method relieves the shear stresses on the fasteners. It conducts the compressive forces of the structure through the post. *Source:* Illustration by Chad Wichers.

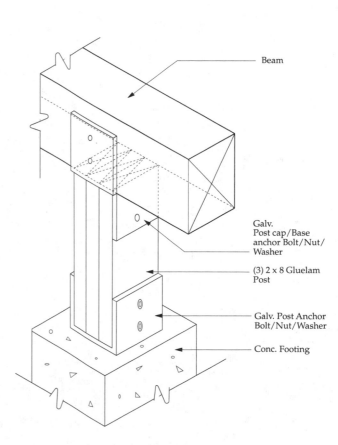

Figure 3.61   Large wood posts can be expensive and are not always readily available. An alternative is the glue-laminated or mechanically fastened "built-up" post. *Source:* Illustration by Chad Wichers.

Beams

The beams are intermediate structural members that transfer the dead loads of the decking joists (if used) and live loads to the post or pier. They can be solid lumber, 4 × 6 or 4 × 8, or like a column, built up of 2× material. Nailing the boards face to face, a common mistake, promotes premature material decay. In fabricating a built up beam, spacers made of treated lumber or plywood are placed between the two or more pieces of 2× material at spacings of 12 to 18 in., depending on the depth of the material. The spacers are glued and/or fastened to the beam members, allowing air circulation between the members and creating a void for water to pass through (see Figure 3.62).

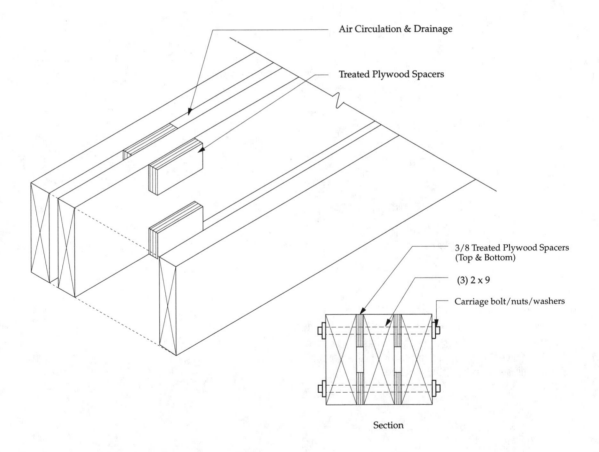

Air Circulation & Drainage

Treated Plywood Spacers

3/8 Treated Plywood Spacers (Top & Bottom)

(3) 2 x 9

Carriage bolt/nuts/washers

Section

Figure 3.62 Similar to built-up posts, beams are often composed of glue-laminated members or are mechanically fastened. Spacers placed between the wood members allow water to drain and air to circulate, reducing potential for decay. *Source:* Illustration by Chad Wichers.

The best method for supporting a beam is to rest it on top of a post, thus using the post to provide the best compressive resistance. This method does raise the profile of the deck, and if this is aesthetically unacceptable, the beams can be bolted through to the side of the column. Side bolting places much of the shear stresses on the fasteners, and if inappropriately sized, the fasteners can suffer metal fatigue, which can result in structural failure. Notching the post and bolting it to the beam is an intermediate solution.

A variety of galvanized metal connectors are designed to form a mechanical connection between the beam and the post (see Figure 3.63). The connectors are designed to be mounted on top of a wood post or to be embedded in the top of a concrete pier if the wood post is eliminated. In using a wood post, it is important that the width of the beam is equal to or greater than the

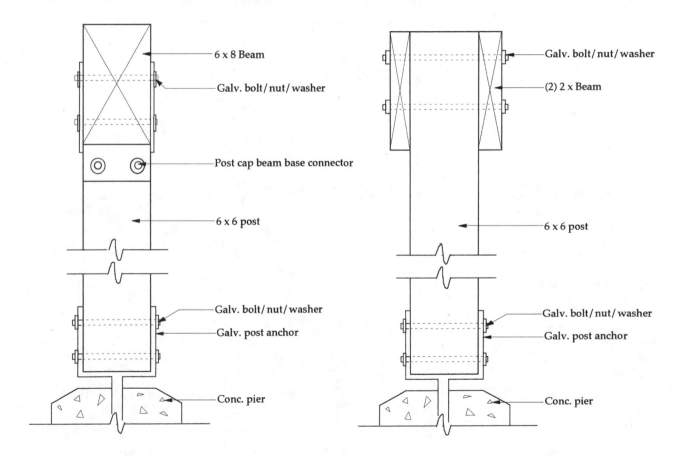

Figure 3.63   The commonly used sandwich beam is less serviceable than the notched post (see Figure 3.60) or the traditional solid post. The loads are transferred to the post through the fasteners, placing severe shear stresses on the bolts. The bolts must be adequately sized. *Source:* Illustration by Chad Wichers.

post so that water does not flow down the face of the beam and into the end grain of the post. If the post is cut, the exposed end grain should be treated with a preservative before the beam is set in place.

Wood post connectors are either H-shaped or a twisted H shape, whereby the direction of the U shapes top and bottom are perpendicular to each other, allowing the bolts to be perpendicular in the respective posts and beam (see Figure 3.61). Each connector has predrilled holes providing locations for carriage or machine bolts. There are also U straps that extend up from the sides of the post and over the top of the beam. Some designers use steel flat bars with predrilled holes for straps and connect one to each side of the beam and the post.

The form of the beam depends on where the point of contact between the posts and the beam is. The following beams are common in deck construction:

Figure 3.64 The ledger is bolted through a structural cladding onto a rim joist, sill top, or bottom plate. Because the bolt penetrates the building skin, it is important that these points be protected. The tuck "Z" flashing prevents water migration between the ledger and the building. *Source:* Illustration by Chad Wichers.

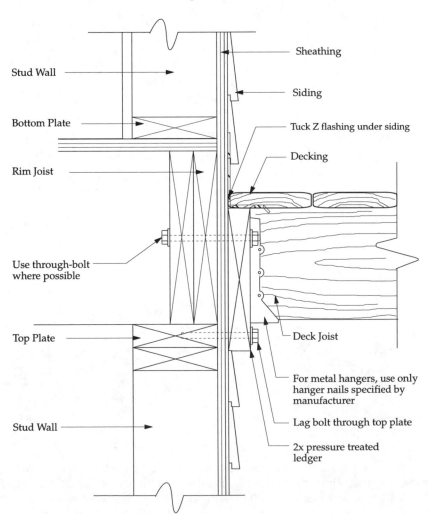

Stud Wall

Bottom Plate

Rim Joist

Use through-bolt where possible

Top Plate

Stud Wall

Sheathing

Siding

Tuck Z flashing under siding

Decking

Deck Joist

For metal hangers, use only hanger nails specified by manufacturer

Lag bolt through top plate

2x pressure treated ledger

1. Simple beam: a single-span beam supported at each end
2. Cantilever beam: supported only on one end
3. Overhanging beam: extends beyond one or more supports
4. Continuous beam: supported by three or more structural members
5. Fixed beam: fixed to supports at each end

Another structural member, a ledger, is not technically a beam but acts in a similar manner. A ledger supports the same loads as a beam, but instead of resting on posts or piers, it is mechanically attached to an existing structure. When the deck extends out from a building, a 2× or 4× member is connected to the existing rim joists or vertical framing (studs). The ledger is attached with two ⅜ in. diameter lag bolts every 24 in. to the rim (band) joist

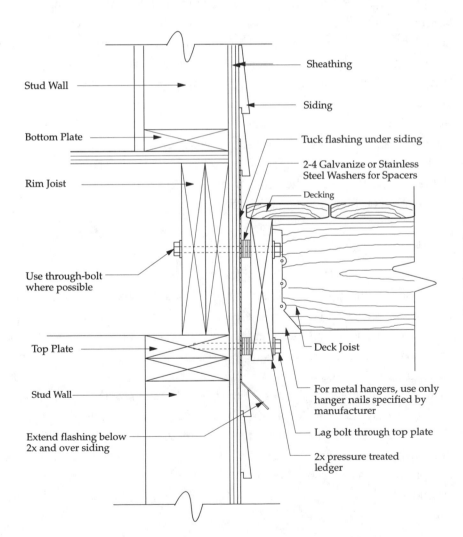

Figure 3.65   Spacers provide an alternative to the method used in Figure 3.64 and are set between the ledger and the flashing to allow air to circulate and water to pass. *Source:* Illustration by Chad Wichers.

or to wall studs, or expansion bolted to the foundation wall; thus, the ledger is continuously mechanically supported. Because the dressed ledger member is only 1½ in. ± thick, little surface area for nailing is provided and the deck nailing must be done very close to the ends or sides of the decking boards, which can cause the boards to split. To resolve this problem, a flat 2 × 4 can be attached flush to the top of the ledger, providing an additional 1½ in. or a total of 3 in. support and nailing area.

In attaching the joists to the ledger, toe nailing should be avoided. The size of the nails required will split the ends of the joists and allow water to collect where it should not. To eliminate a toe nail connection, joist hangers can be nailed to the ledger to receive the joists. An alternative method that reduces but does not eliminate toe nailing is to select a ledger 2 in. taller than the joists, nail or screw a 2 × 2 in. piece of wood (cleat) flush to the bottom of the ledger, and lay a bead of sealant at the joint to prevent water infiltration. The joist can now rest on the cleat. The joist will still have to be toe nailed into the ledger, but smaller nails can be used, thus avoiding the splitting. This method should be used only if other options are not possible, because water will sit on the cleat, causing debris and fungi to accumulate, and most of the loads will be supported by the cleat. Whatever the method of connecting the joists, the ledger should also receive a Z flashing strip that tucks under the wall siding and runs 90 degrees out over the top and 90 degrees down the face of the ledger to prevent water from penetrating the rim joist or sill (see Figures 3.64 and 3.65).

Joists

The joist, in the platform method of framing, transfers the live and dead loads of the decking to the beams. Joists are positioned perpendicular to the beams and can either be set on top of the beams or hung flush with the top of the beams with joist hangers (see Figures 3.66, 3.67, and 3.68). The first method relies on the integrity of the beam to transfer the loads; the second method depends on the integrity of the connector, the joist hanger, to transfer the loads to the beams (see Figures 3.66 and 3.67). The spacing of the joists is determined by the span capability, which is determined by the dimension of the decking. Typical joist spacing ranges from 16 in. OC to 24 in. OC when supporting ⁵⁄₄ in. or 2× decking. The first method elevates the joist, increasing the profile of the deck by the vertical dimension of the joist lying above the beam (see Figure 3.66). The connectors used in this application are hurricane

Figure 3.66   This accessible ramp, as specified by the Americans with Disabilities Act (ADA), is framed with curved joists supported by sandwich beams with blocking set between joists. *Source:* University of Washington Design/Build Studio, instructors Daniel Winterbottom and Luanne Smith, 1998.

Figure 3.67   Framing a deck floor that covers a water cistern. These angled joists are hung flush with built-up beams, creating a lower profile than the traditional platform system would allow. *Source:* University of Washington Design/Build Studio, instructors Daniel Winterbottom and Luanne Smith, 1999.

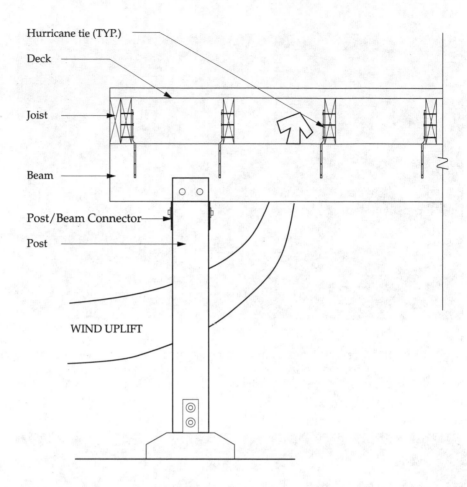

Hurricane tie (TYP.)

Deck

Joist

Beam

Post/Beam Connector

Post

WIND UPLIFT

Figure 3.68   To counter the forces of wind, metal fasteners, called ties, connect the joists to beams to provide resistance. Ties provide greater strength than toe nailing. *Source:* Illustration by Chad Wichers.

ties, twist straps that connect the joist to the beam in order to resist uplift by wind pressure (see Figure 3.68).

If the joists are set flush with the beam, a joist hanger or ledger is employed. The joist hanger, a galvanized metal stirrup, is nailed to the beam, the joist is placed into the **U**-shaped stirrup, and the stirrup is nailed to the joist.

Joists can span long distances in relation to their vertical dimension, but twisting or curving is a potential problem. To counter this tendency, solid wood blocking, of the same dimensions as the joists, or 1 × 2 wood or metal bridging is placed between the joists at the midpoint of the spans and nailed to each member to resist movement (see Figure 3.67).

Another common problem to be avoided in attaching the decking to the joists is nailing close to the end grain of the decking boards, which can cause the boards to split. When the joints are staggered, this is hard to avoid. If a

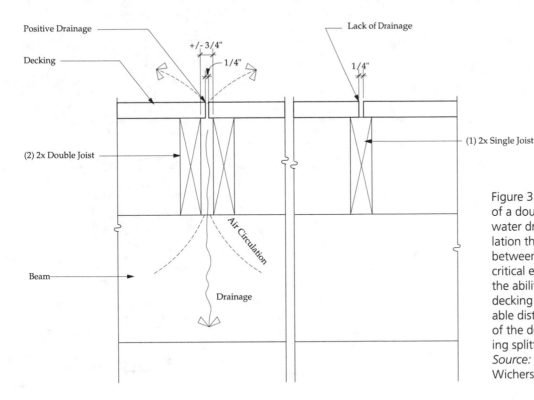

Positive Drainage

Decking

+/- 3/4"

1/4"

Lack of Drainage

1/4"

(1) 2x Single Joist

(2) 2x Double Joist

Air Circulation

Beam

Drainage

Figure 3.69 The advantages of a double joist system are water drainage and air circulation through the joists and between the decking at the critical end grain edges and the ability to connect the decking to the joist a reasonable distance from the ends of the deck boards, eliminating splitting at the ends. *Source:* Illustration by Chad Wichers.

pattern requires the decking to change directions at a particular point or if joints line up in a running pattern, a double joist system can be employed. Instead of using one joist, which provides only ¾ in. of bearing and forces the nail to be driven at the edge of the decking board, a double joist can be added. If a 2× spacer is used between the two 2× members (see Figure 3.69), the nails at the end of the decking boards can be set approximately 1½ in. back from the edge. This system also allows good drainage and ventilation for the decking end grain, instead of permitting water to be trapped by the joist below as in the single joist method.

In orienting both beams and joists, the members should be designed to orient vertically to the cross section's longitudinal axis. All board lumber has a "crook," a bend that is counter to the greatest dimension. In some members this is obvious, in others it may be more difficult to see. When the joists are placed, it is important to orient the "crowned" side up. This allows the weight of the structure to provide a counterresistance that will straighten the crown instead of increasing pressure on the natural curve as it would if the member were placed crown-side down (see Figures 3.70 A and B).

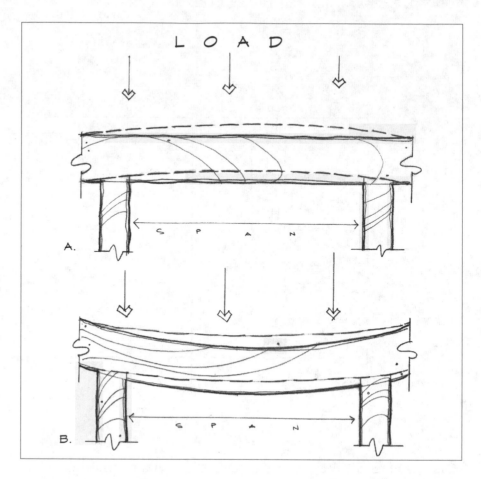

Figures 3.70 A and B   All boards have a crown, a bow in the longitudinal direction along the thin edge. In the field it may or may not be clearly visible. Once found, the crown should be oriented up to the decking or structural member above, providing greater resistance to the loads. If reversed, the member will tend to sag. *Source:* Illustration by Jody Estes.

Decking

The decking, which provides a usable surface on which to stand and walk, spans the joists or beams, transferring live weights to the structural members below. The span is determined by the spacing of the joists below and is calculated to the size and span capabilities of the decking material (see Figure 3.3, page 61). There are a number of options in specifying the decking material. Any material under ⁵⁄₄ in. should be avoided for exposed decking applications. The material choices include ⁵⁄₄ × 6 in., 2 × 4 in., and 2 × 6 in. The ⁵⁄₄ or 2× material used for decking should be no greater than 6 in. in width, owing to a propensity to warp in wider boards. In some public structures thicker material, such as 2 or 3 in., is used in the plank-and-beam method, and as the thickness of the decking material increases, so too does the spacing of the joists or beams. A gap of ⅛ to ¼ in. should be maintained between the decking boards, depending on their moisture content and subsequent shrinking, to allow proper drainage.

Because the decking, rails, and seating are the most visual elements of the deck structure, appearance grade materials are often selected to build them. The bark side (see Figures 3.71 A and B) should be oriented facing up so that any cupping that occurs will not deflect water down, thus allowing proper drainage between the decking materials. Decking is most frequently laid in flat with the thinnest dimension in the vertical orientation; however, as the spans increase, it is possible to lay the decking with the thickest dimension vertical position and widen the beam or joist spacing. Decking oriented in this manner has an increased resistance to bouncing or sagging, but the amount of decking material needed will greatly increase, as well as the material costs. When this method is used, ¼ to ⅜ in. spacers of treated marine grade plywood or solid treated material should be placed at intervals of 2 to 3 ft between the decking members to increase stability.

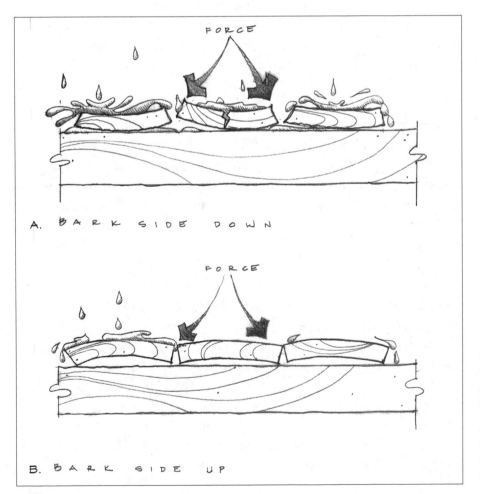

A. BARK SIDE DOWN

B. BARK SIDE UP

Figures 3.71 A and B   When the "barkside" is oriented down, the boards cup up, entrapping water; conversely, when oriented up, the boards will shed water and, with live weights, will tend to flatten out over time. *Source:* Illustration by Jody Estes.

This method also requires toe nailing the decking to the structural material below, and replacement of single boards becomes very difficult after installation.

Because the decking material is not only the most exposed material used in deck construction but also takes the most abuse over time, it is often the first material to deteriorate. Frequent applications of preservative treatments will extend the life span of the decking material. When possible, butt joints in the decking should be avoided. Where they are used, end grains are subjected to holding moisture and the life of the deck will be shorter, with the chance of deterioration spreading to the structure below. The double joist system, described earlier, will reduce moisture entrapment (see Figure 3.69).

Another cause of deck failure is the migration of water through the nail holes, particularly when the nails lose their withdrawal resistance and pop up. These openings leave a clear path for water to penetrate below the effective treatment penetration zone, causing the material to degrade from the inside out. The rate of withdrawal in smooth-shank nails is quite high in areas of heavy foot traffic, and spiral-groove or ring-shank nails or screws are recommended for attaching decking boards in these conditions. The length of the connecting mechanism will also affect withdrawal; the fastener should be 3 in. (10 d) or greater when securing 1 in. thick decking, and 3½ in. (16 d) or greater for 1½ in. boards. If edge nailing cannot be avoided, all holes should be predrilled to minimize splitting at the ends of the boards.

When the deck is freestanding and is not laterally held rigid through a connection to an existing structure, the vertical structural members should be braced to remain stable. In a building, the framing is tied together with sheathing, providing lateral stability. In deck construction, the structural members are exposed, and in lieu of sheathing, bracing (diagonal cross members) are used to resist racking and possible structural failure. For high structures—decks sited on sloping lots requiring long posts, for example—the need for bracing is critical. Any decks greater than 5 ft in height should be braced, particularly at the corners.

Bracing can take a number of forms (see Figure 3.72), and in most cases the simple Y type bracing should be sufficient for standard post-to-beam connections. This method of bracing, depending on the elevations, has an advantage in allowing easy access below the deck. Where the Y type of bracing is impractical or when the structure is designed with long beam spans or tall posts, X cross bracing can be installed at alternate bays, although some decks may require bracing at every bay for structural support. If the height of the posts exceeds 14 ft, two X braces or K braces, one on top of the other, may be required, and an engineer should be consulted.

If the length of the bracing is 8 ft or less, 2 × 4s are usually adequate; for longer unsupported lengths, 2 × 6s are recommended. All connections should be to the main framing, with a minimum of ⅜ in. bolts used for fastening. The number of bolts should be minimized to prevent moisture entrapment, and end grain exposure to water should also be minimized. Both end grain and predrilled holes can be treated before attachment.

Stairs

Most decks include at least some stairs, and in many cases the stairs are a feature equal in visual impact to the decking. If the stairs include more than two risers (vertical steps), most codes require at least one railing at the side of the run (see Figure 3.81C, page 125). All risers and treads (horizontal steps) should be of a consistent dimension within any run, and preferably within the whole design (see Figure 3.73). If the design incorporates lumber of standard dimensions, there will be less waste and greater efficiency in material use. For example, a stair tread of 11½ in. can be created from two 2 × 6s or three 2 × 4s, and a rise of 5½ in. can be achieved from a single 2 × 6. When nonstandard lumber is used, the members will have to be ripped (cut perpendicular to the grain), and the cut surfaces will need a field-applied treatment. Factory-applied preservative treatments are always preferable.

Whatever the dimensions of the boards, the material for the treads should not be less than ⁵⁄₄ in., and 2× stock is most commonly used. When the riser is closed, the covering material can be thinner, typically ¾ in., because it receives very little live or dead load; it is used to prevent toes from going under the tread and for the aesthetic effect. The tread and riser boards are supported by a structural framing member called a stringer. A stringer is fabricated from a large board, often a treated 2 × 12 or 2 × 14, that has been cut to form a stepped pattern on which the tread boards are attached (see Figure 3.74).

Each stringer is identical to the others and must be placed vertically plumb and horizontally level. The number of stringers required depends on the width of the stairs; however, if fewer than three are used, sagging can occur even on a stair with a width as short as 2½ ft. The boards are attached in the same manner as the decking, with either nails or screws. The stringer is attached to either the rim joist, beam, or blocking attached between the posts

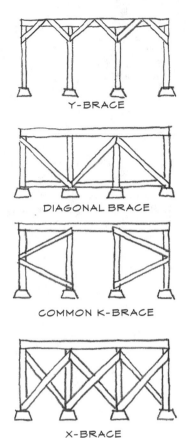

Y-BRACE

DIAGONAL BRACE

COMMON K-BRACE

X-BRACE

Figure 3.72 Bracing is configured to resist lateral sway. The most common are the Y, X, and K braces. Bracing members should be placed with end grain oriented down or parallel with the post, and bolt connections should be minimized to prevent moisture infiltration. *Source:* Illustration by Daniel Winterbottom.

Figure 3.73   The stringer connects the level of the deck to the grade, for the installation of stair risers and treads. There are a number of stringer-to-framing connections, including connections to the rim joist, to the blocking between the joists, and to the beam. *Source:* Illustration by Chad Wichers.

Figure 3.74   Stair stringer connected to a ledger with a joist hanger at the upper end, and to a lower joist that also supports a landing between stair runs.

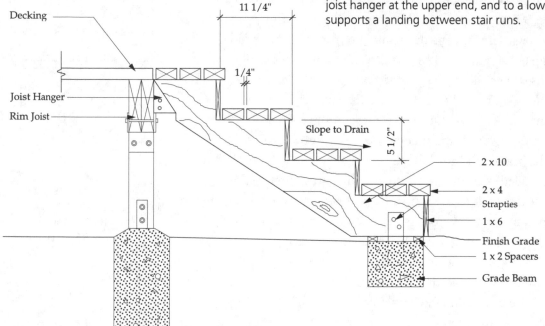

(see Figures 3.73 and 3.74). Joist hangers or other metal connectors can be employed to connect the upper stringer end to the joist or blocking. The lower stringer end should rest on a concrete beam foundation or on footings below each stringer. This prevents direct contact with the ground and keeps the stairs from settling. The stringer should be attached to the footing with metal straps or tied down to prevent horizontal movement or uplift caused by wind (see Figures 3.75 A–C).

Figures 3.75 A–C   Options for resting the stringer at grade. (A) This option is the least permanent and is prone to settlement. (B) Provides a good connection and the layout of connections allows some flexibility. (C) Provides a good connection, and with a retrofit bolt can be installed after the pad is poured, allowing the greatest flexibility. *Source:* Illustration by Chad Wichers.

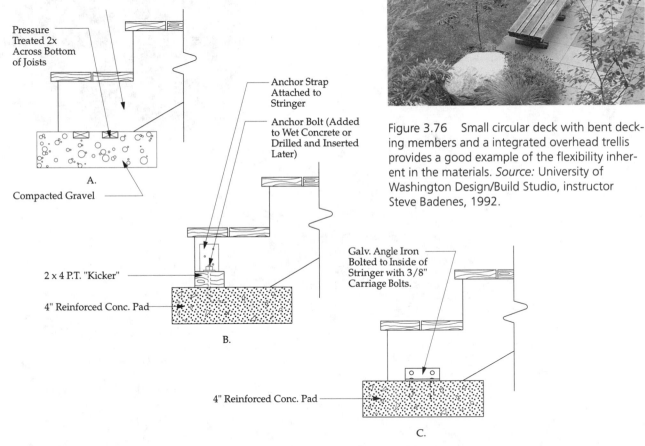

Pressure Treated 2x Across Bottom of Joists

Compacted Gravel

A.

Anchor Strap Attached to Stringer

Anchor Bolt (Added to Wet Concrete or Drilled and Inserted Later)

2 x 4 P.T. "Kicker"

4" Reinforced Conc. Pad

B.

Galv. Angle Iron Bolted to Inside of Stringer with 3/8" Carriage Bolts.

4" Reinforced Conc. Pad

C.

Figure 3.76   Small circular deck with bent decking members and a integrated overhead trellis provides a good example of the flexibility inherent in the materials. *Source:* University of Washington Design/Build Studio, instructor Steve Badenes, 1992.

Seating

Built-in benches, because they are often incorporated into the structural framing with the posts serving as the vertical supports from which the bench supports are cantilevered, must be planned during the design phase (see Figure 3.76).

A reasonable amount of surface area is required to attach the bench supports to the post, and often the posts are sized as 6 × 6s or as independent 2 × 8 mem-

Figure 3.77 A pressure-treated wood framing structure and plastic lumber slats form this continuous bench. University of Washington Design/Build Studio, instructors Daniel Winterbottom and Luanne Smith, 1999.

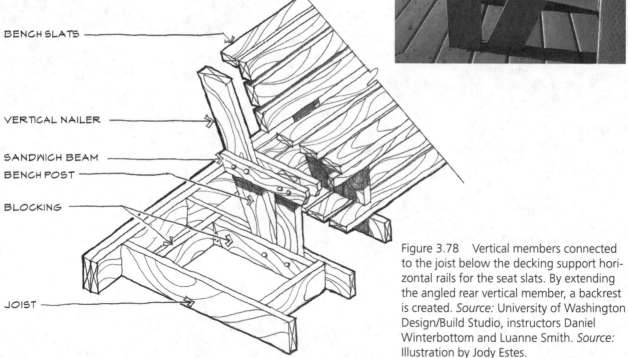

BENCH SLATS

VERTICAL NAILER

SANDWICH BEAM
BENCH POST

BLOCKING

JOIST

Figure 3.78 Vertical members connected to the joist below the decking support horizontal rails for the seat slats. By extending the angled rear vertical member, a backrest is created. *Source:* University of Washington Design/Build Studio, instructors Daniel Winterbottom and Luanne Smith. *Source:* Illustration by Jody Estes.

bers extended up from the structural framing (see Figures 3.77 and 3.78). These structural members can be notched to receive the frame member supporting the bench slats and ripped to 4 in. or angled slightly above the seating to support a backrest. The bench structure can be banded with 2 × 4s with 2 × 6 cross members supporting the bench slats (see Figure 3.84, page 126).

Railings

Deck railings can be quite complex, such as those with ornate features like turned balustrades and finials, or can be designed as very simple and functional elements. The illustrations give a sampling of some options, and the following discussion provides some basic principles that should be followed regardless of the design (see Figures 3.79 and 3.80).

Most local building codes regulate railing heights and maximum balustrade openings when required by code (see Figures 3.81 A–C). Generally, openings between balustrades or pickets should be no greater than 4 in., and a 42 in. railing height is required if the deck is more than 18 in. above finished grade (see Figures 3.81 A–C). Before designing a railing, the local building codes should be consulted. It is common to extend the posts up through the decking as vertical supports for the top, bottom, and middle rails, inasmuch as

Figure 3.79   Two types of decks are incorporated into the south-facing side of this Seattle residence with the upper deck providing protection in inclement weather for those below. In the lower deck an open railing system allows light to enter into the covered space and provides maximum visibility without sacrificing security. The upper deck uses a solid railing providing greater privacy. Note the natural rough-hewn columns that support the bearing beam above.

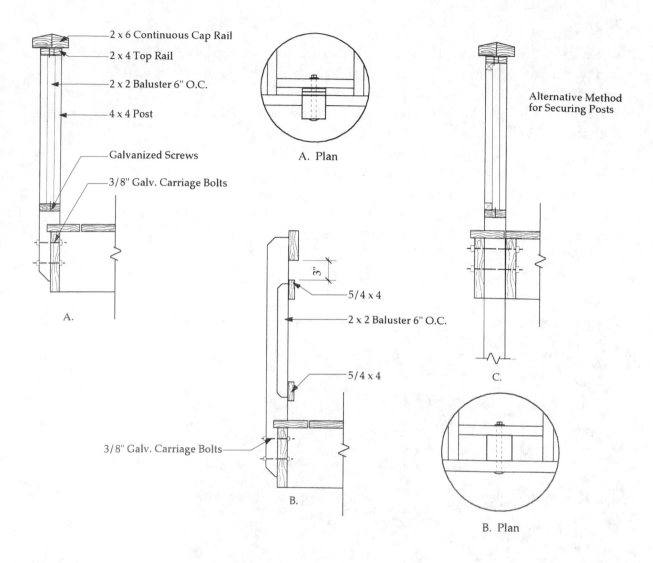

2 x 6 Continuous Cap Rail

2 x 4 Top Rail

2 x 2 Baluster 6" O.C.

4 x 4 Post

Galvanized Screws

3/8" Galv. Carriage Bolts

A.

A. Plan

Alternative Method
for Securing Posts

3"

5/4 x 4

2 x 2 Baluster 6" O.C.

5/4 x 4

3/8" Galv. Carriage Bolts

B.

C.

B. Plan

Figure 3.80   There are a number of options for connecting the rail to the deck. In system C, the rails can be attached to posts extending up through the decking or to post extensions attached to the beam or rim joist. *Source:* Illustration by Chad Wichers.

the full length of the posts is used to resist the rail load (see Figure 3.84). When 4 × 4 posts are used to support the rails, the post spacing should not exceed 6 ft, because the rails transfer the dead loads of the balustrades and rails to the posts and spacing greater than 6 ft can cause the rails to sag. If the posts cannot be extended through the decking, they can be bolted to the beams or joist framing to support the rails; however, this again places the stresses on the metal fastener (see Figures 3.80 and 3.82).

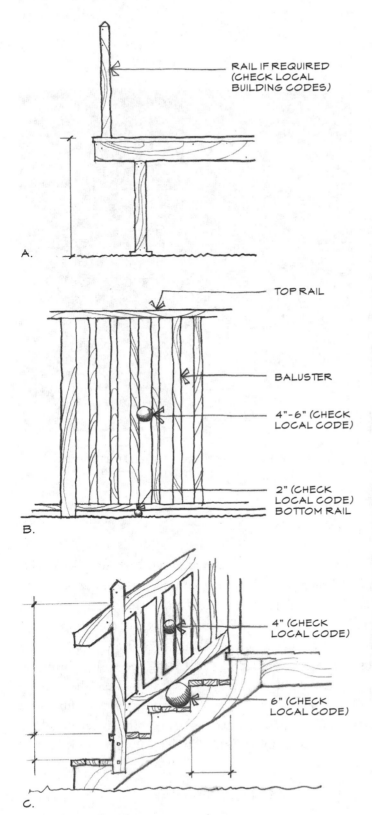

A.

RAIL IF REQUIRED
(CHECK LOCAL
BUILDING CODES)

TOP RAIL

BALUSTER

4"-6" (CHECK
LOCAL CODE)

2" (CHECK
LOCAL CODE)
BOTTOM RAIL

B.

4" (CHECK
LOCAL CODE)

6" (CHECK
LOCAL CODE)

C.

Figures 3.81 A–C   (A) The deck height is the determining factor for required railings. In most parts of the country, if the deck is 30 in. off the ground, a railing is required. (B) The distance between vertical railing members is determined by the diameter of a ball passing through the space. A 4 to 6 in. diameter is used by many codes. Some jurisdictions also require a height of 2 in. or less between the bottom rail and the decking surface. (C) The stair railings, treads and risers are also controlled by code. Rail heights range from 30 to 38 in. measured from the front of riser. A 7 to 8 in. maximum rise and a 9 to 11 in. minimum tread is standard in most codes. The distance between vertical members on the stairs is the same as for a deck, and a 6 in. maximum from the bottom rail to the tread is usually required. *Source:* Illustration by Jody Estes.

Figure 3.82   The end posts for the deck also support the railings. These horizontal rails create a strong line, but their design encourages climbing and they may not be usable for high decks or playground settings.

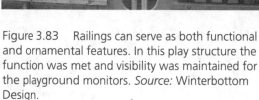

Figure 3.83   Railings can serve as both functional and ornamental features. In this play structure the function was met and visibility was maintained for the playground monitors. *Source:* Winterbottom Design.

Figure 3.84   A deck with railings, arbor, and planter boxes illustrates an integrated approach to this structure.

RELATED SPECIFICATIONS
06050—Fasteners and
          Adhesives
06100—Rough Carpentry
06130—Heavy Timber
          Construction
06170—Prefabricated
          Structural Wood
06200—Finish Carpentry
06300—Wood Treatment

A notched railing should be avoided, as it has a tendency to split. All railing members should be particularly strong and all connections firm and rigid, especially when the deck is at a high elevation. The railing provides a place for leaning and is often used to as a barrier to contain children.

A rail cap not only provides a horizontal surface to lean on or to place things on, but also prevents water from penetrating the end grain of the posts. The rail cap should be angled to shed water away from the decking (see Figure 3.80). The cap also provides an opportunity to install fiberoptic strips or other forms of lighting in a routed channel on the underside of the cap or behind a horizontal member below the cap for recessed lighting effects.

ARBORS AND PERGOLAS

INTRODUCTION

Arbors and pergolas, originally designed as shade structures, were common in the warm climates of Mediterranean countries such as Italy and Spain (see Figure 3.85).

They appeared throughout Europe as traveling explorers returned to their home countries and replicated what they had found abroad in the Mediterranean countries. Spanish conquistadors sailing to the Americas incorporated elements of their European gardens into the native forms and materials they encountered. Shade-providing pergolas and arbors began to define the plazas and courtyards of the developing European towns in

Figure 3.85 As this medieval woodcut illustrates, ornamental pergolas have long been used to provide shade and used as climbing frames for fruit bearing vines. *Source:* From *Decorating Eden,* edited by Elizabeth Wilkinson and Marjorie Henderson © 1992. Published by Chronicle Books, San Francisco. Used with permission.

Mexico, the Caribbean, and parts of South America. These structures offered not just shade, but a place to display the brilliant flowers of bougainvillea and climbing roses and to cultivate fruiting vines. Because wood was scarce in some parts of the New World, a combination of masonry columns with wood cross members were built; in other areas wood was abundant, and there these structures were built primarily of wood (see Figure 3.86).

Most pergolas are freestanding structures, often linear in form and at times creating a visual or literal connection between two spaces or structures. In some cases they function as transparent outdoor rooms, with open walls and a translucent roof. Most arbors, on the other hand, define a single space, frame a view, or serve as an extension of an existing structure, serving as a transition space or room, linking the large structure to the landscape. The siting of a pergola or arbor is often related to entry features; it may be designed as an extension of a structure into the landscape (arbor) or as an independent structure (pergola) to be discovered. Many pergolas ring an open courtyard and offer a formal, almost ceremonial circulation route about a civic space. Most of these structures are sited on level ground. They can be stepped if

Figure 3.86 Using a traditional system of posts and vigas, landscape architect Bill Hays has designed carved pine columns to support a wood beam and rough-hewn logs to form an arbor. The structure, supported by a straw bale wall at the rear, creates a shaded outdoor room, the central feature of the patio. *Source:* Photo by Bill Hays.

sited on an incline, but stairs or ramping will have to be incorporated, and these are relatively rare. In addition to providing shade, the design of an arbor offers opportunities to create integrated seating. Through its placement, form, and scale, an arbor can announce entry into a space and provide a welcoming destination point. The drama of passing through an arbor used as an entry can be enhanced through lighting. Sconce lighting or hanging fixtures may be attached to the overhead structure. As with fences, the styles and characters of arbors and pergolas cover a broad range. Because these structures are by nature architectonic and are often attached to or related visually to an existing structure, designs related to a historical period or regional vernacular are common. Many of these structures are designed to facilitate vines, and care should be taken to size members so that the plants can twine or attach to them. All members must be sized for the weight of mature plants (see Figure 3.87). Species such as wisteria may need extra support from steel pipes or tubes or from oversized wood members. The siting, sizing, and connections of an arbor or pergola may fall within municipal regulations for structures, and all building codes should be checked before the design process begins.

Figure 3.87   Masonry columns support timber beams at the Brooklyn Botanical Garden. The timbers are sized to support the substantial loads of fully mature wisteria vines.

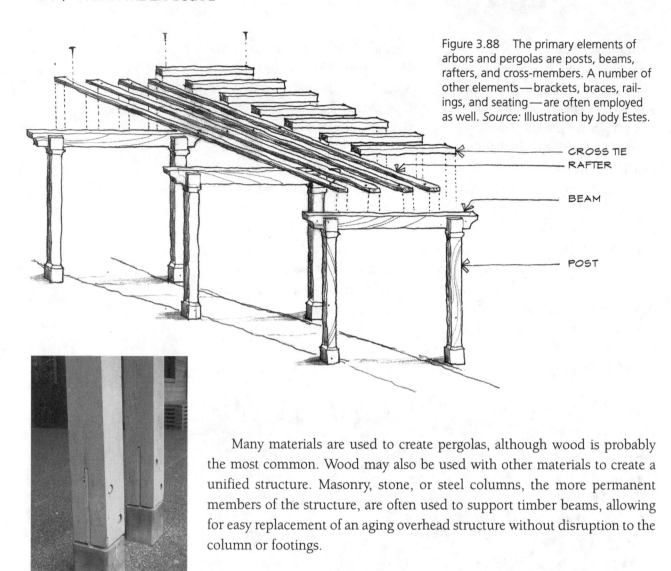

Figure 3.88   The primary elements of arbors and pergolas are posts, beams, rafters, and cross-members. A number of other elements—brackets, braces, railings, and seating—are often employed as well. *Source:* Illustration by Jody Estes.

CROSS TIE
RAFTER
BEAM
POST

Figure 3.89   These custom designed stainless steel post anchors are both aesthetically appealing and provide adequate distance between the end grain of the post and the ground plane, reducing water infiltration and the potential for build up of fungi and molds. A slot cut into the post base receives the tongue of the anchor and bolts provide a mechanical connection.

Many materials are used to create pergolas, although wood is probably the most common. Wood may also be used with other materials to create a unified structure. Masonry, stone, or steel columns, the more permanent members of the structure, are often used to support timber beams, allowing for easy replacement of an aging overhead structure without disruption to the column or footings.

STRUCTURE

The primary structural elements used to build a pergola or arbor include the footings, posts or columns, beams, and rafters (see Figure 3.88). The footing and the post attachment are similar to those used in fence construction; however, they may be significantly greater in width to support the dead weight of the beam, rafters, and plant material. If the post is wood, post anchors provide separation from the footing and allow for air circulation below (see Figure 3.89). The post can be a solid timber, usually a 4 × 6, 6 × 6, or 4 × 8, or can be laminated using two or more 2× boards with spacers. The top should be angled, rounded, or capped to shed water. It is best from a structural standpoint that the beam sits atop the post and the stresses are conducted through compression. An option with a solid post is to notch the post on both sides, creating a bench to set a built-up sandwich beam (see Figures 3.90 and 3.93). If the column is not notched and a sandwich beam is used, the stresses are shear and carried by the fasteners.

The beam spans the distance between the posts and can be oriented parallel or perpendicular to the post alignment (see Figures 3.90 A and B). The beam can be either a solid member or a built-up sandwich beam, again with spacers and with the members glued and/or bolted together. The size of the beam depends on the span or distance between columns. Thus, if the posts

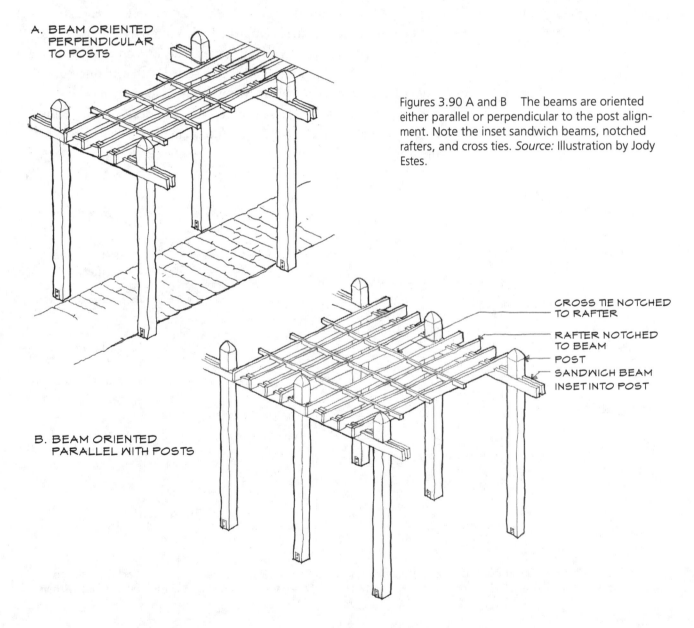

A. BEAM ORIENTED PERPENDICULAR TO POSTS

B. BEAM ORIENTED PARALLEL WITH POSTS

CROSS TIE NOTCHED TO RAFTER

RAFTER NOTCHED TO BEAM

POST

SANDWICH BEAM INSET INTO POST

Figures 3.90 A and B   The beams are oriented either parallel or perpendicular to the post alignment. Note the inset sandwich beams, notched rafters, and cross ties. *Source:* Illustration by Jody Estes.

are spaced 10 ft on center, the beam must be sized to span 10 ft. The beam should be properly doweled, bolted, or strapped to the post. As with free-standing decks, and depending on the height and spacing of the posts, bracing may be incorporated into a pergola or arbor to resist the racking of the frame. A Y brace should suffice in most situations, and in a timber frame system this is often detailed as a highly crafted feature within the framing (see Figure 3.91).

The rafters can either be set atop the beams and stabilized with metal connectors or be attached to and set between and flush with the top of the beam (see Figures 3.92 and 3.95 B). In the second option the end grain of the rafter butts to the side of the beam, which can entrap water; this method is discouraged, as the longevity of the rafters can be compromised (see Figures 3.94 and 3.95 A). These joints can be sealed with caulking but will need ongoing maintenance to ensure that water is adequately repelled. End nailing through the beam into the rafter should be avoided. A metal connector such as a joist hanger is a better option, although not particularly aesthetically pleasing.

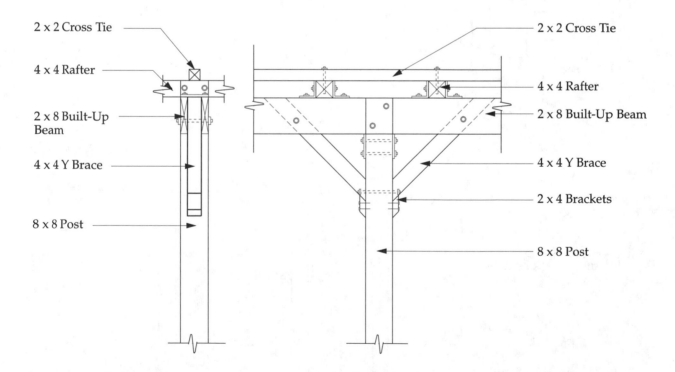

Figure 3.91   Pergolas and arbors may require bracing to resist lateral forces. The post/beam configuration suggests the method of bracing to be used. Here the Y bracing is sandwiched between the beams. *Source:* Illustration by Chad Wichers.

Figure 3.92   A steel fastener connects the beam to the rafter in this pergola in New York's Central Park. The post is notched to receive the sandwich beam, and the machine bolts at the bottom of the steel connector tie the sandwich beam through the post tongue, securing the structure to the post.

Figure 3.93   Beams and rafters of the same dimension create a dramatic detail. The extended overhangs and rounded motif create a focal point.

Figure 3.94   Lead flashing protects the joints of this arched box beam. The mortised and tenoned rafters are set into the arch.

When the rafters are placed atop the beam they should be extended beyond the face of the beam and detailed to shed water. This can be achieved by angling the ends or by using a rounded detail (see Figures 3.93 and 3.95 A and B). These members can also be notched around the beam, adding increased stability to the structure. Once the rafters are set, additional cross members can be gridded, either atop or through the rafters, although the sizes of the cross members will depend on the span and capability of the wood.

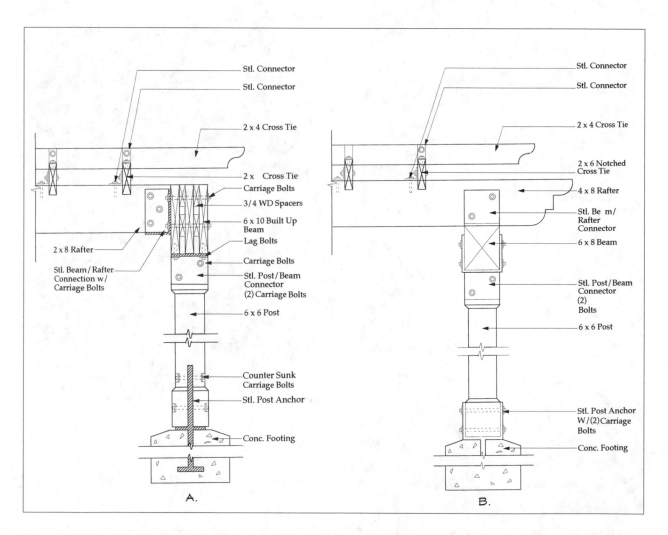

Figures 3.95 A and B These two details provide different options. In (B) the rafter sits flush with the top of the built-up beam in (B) the post base connector is placed into a saw cut of the column, in (A) the column is set in the base bracket. *Source:* Illustration by Chad Wichers.

FREESTANDING STRUCTURES:
GAZEBOS, PAVILIONS, AND CABINS

The range of wood structures designed as elements in and related to the landscape is extensive and varied throughout the cultures of the world. From the simple thatched teahouses in Japan, with their long verandahs welcoming the traveler, to the boat houses found at the large lakes in America's urban parks of the 1800s, wood structures have been a part of the design vocabulary of landscape architects.

For centuries designers have been creating independent structures in the landscape as viewing points in the garden or as destinations to be discovered. Gazebos in the seventeenth century were originally small towerlike structures sited within the walls of an enclosed garden or in a corner, providing a junction where portions of a wall or fence converged. From an observation pavilion, views either out beyond or facing into the garden were possible. These structures, built with side walls, doors, and windows, were quite substantial. In comparison, the contemporary gazebo is an open structure with timber or carved posts, low infill latticework and built-in benches, often centered within the garden.

The *t'ing,* prevalent in the Chinese garden, and the teahouse in the Japanese garden provide a function similar to that of the gazebo. Both small, relatively open structures provide a focal point in the landscape. The Chinese structures are traditionally raised with large rounded posts and massive wood beams supporting a curved, sweeping tile-clad roof with deep eaves (see Figure 3.96). Although some are enclosed, most are encircled with a low balustrade, providing seating and additional opportunities for ornamentation. Japanese teahouses, on the other hand, tend to be simple timber-framed structures. Instead of the turned columns found in the *t'ing,* the teahouse features natural log posts, and rough-hewn beams and rafters support a thatched or wood-shingled roof. Wood benches, anchored to the columns and backed by plastered walls, provide seating and enclosures from which the garden beyond is viewed. A teahouse may be built on piles at the water's edge; its form is replicated in the reflection when viewed from afar.

Throughout the eighteenth century the image of the *t'ing* became familiar to Westerners on imported ceramic ware. These fanciful, exotic forms of garden architecture then began to appear in country gardens and city parks.

Figure 3.96   A true timber frame Chinese structure reveals joinery as an integral part of the aesthetic.

As the colonial empires spread, so too did their borrowing of architectural influences, which were liberally interpreted. From Persian palaces to Turkish *koshks,* later evolving into the French *kiosk,* such influences were found in every corner of the globe. In America, pavilions and gazebos, influenced by the older Dutch-English forms, reflected a more conservative approach. Although some designers such as Thomas Jefferson followed their curiosities, mimicking Chinese woodworking, as evidenced in the Chinese balustrade incorporated into a gazebo in Colonial Williamsburg, Virginia, American forms never became as fanciful as their European counterparts. In the nineteenth century, American gardens formally laid out in the Dutch or English style were being influenced by the "return to nature movement," a reaction to the industrialization of the landscape and complementing the Victorian sensibility for craftwork and ornamention. The small garden pavilions, now built of natural wood members, with logs for posts and latticed roofs and rails of limbs and branches joined with mortise and tenons (see Figures 3.97 and 3.98). The Gothic pattern books popular at the time were also influential, and a genre of structures honoring the Carpenter's Gothic appeared, memorable for their rich display of scrollwork, brackets, finials, and carved rafter tails.

Figure 3.97   A focal point in Colonial Williamsburg, Virginia, the "Chinese" balustrade and latticed walls of the gazebo allow cooling garden breezes to enter, offering a welcoming respite from the hot summers. *Source:* From *Decorating Eden,* edited by Elizabeth Wilkinson and Marjorie Henderson © 1992. Published by Chronicle Books, San Francisco. Used with permission.

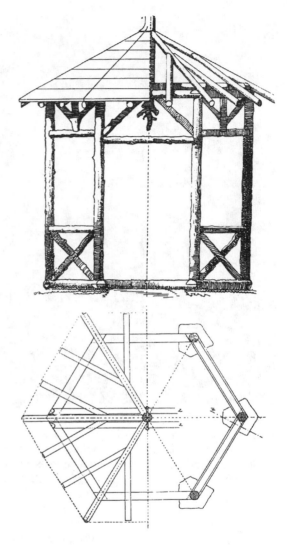

Figure 3.98   This rusticated version of the gazebo uses a simple pole framing method to create what was once a very popular form in the American landscape. *Source:* From *Decorating Eden,* edited by Elizabeth Wilkinson and Marjorie Henderson © 1992. Published by Chronicle Books, San Francisco. Used with permission.

Even today the gazebo retains its popularity, being adopted for outdoor classrooms or as notice boards in village squares. Many New England and Midwestern town commons feature an oversized gazebo (see Figure 3.108, page 155). The form is reinterpreted in the Southwest, where extensively carved columns support rough hewn poles (vigas) to provide shade and a

Figures 3.99 A and B   (A) An elaborate belvedere reminiscent of a Swiss cottage on the grounds of the Marshe-Billings-Rockefeller Mansion and National Historical Park in Woodstock, Vermont. Note the extensive eaves and the detailing on the brackets and railings. This is a good example of how the carpenter's craft can transform a simple box into a little jewel. (B) Notched beams and hidden hardware make this small entry structure a wonderful example of the simple beauty and direct approach inherent in timber frame construction.

place to rest (see Figure 3.87, page 129). As modern landscape architects return, as Thomas Church did, to revisit traditional garden forms, much can be learned from these rich examples of wood construction.

Pavilions, although similar in layout and form to the gazebo, evolved from the tent structures used in Eastern countries as garden shelters. Popular in France in the eighteenth century, the pavilion was used for gathering, as a retreat from the formality of the palace, or as a guest house, often for a mistress (see Figure 3.99 B). Later, the sides and walls were removed, and it became a large, open-air wood structure, a common feature in Victorian public parks, used for dances, concerts, and picnics.

Related in scale to the pavilions are the summer houses. These houses, built by the newly rising middle class who acquired and restored the old country estates, provided shade and a resting place as their owners strolled their grounds.

Landscape wood structures are found not only behind the garden wall; some impressive examples of structures integrated into the land are found in our national forests and parks and in state and county parks across the country. Ranging from simple shed-roofed shelters built of logs to wonderful stone and timber frame cabins and visitor centers, erected during the Federal Works Progress Administration (WPA) of the 1930s, these structures celebrate the integral qualities of wood as a building material. The use of stone at the base grounds the structure in the earth, and the diminishing scale of the wood members, as it rises, breaks down the scale so that the structure does not dominate the space (see Figures 1.12 A and B, page 18).

Many modern examples of wood structures integrated into rural and urban settings can be found in our contemporary landscape. The wood structure by Fay Jones at the Crosbie Arboretum in Mississippi and the pergola by the Halvorson Company at Post Office Square in Boston are exemplary.

Th following sections provide some basic principles for designing these various structures. Before designing a structure, whether a pavilion, play structure, or tree house, a structural system must be chosen. The system must represent the design intent, function, expression, and contextual fit and must meet any cost constraints.

There are two related structural systems that are commonly used and a third that is less commonly employed in exterior structures that are open and exposed to the elements, but is most frequently employed in house and commercial construction.

The first system, pole construction, relies on vertical post members, poles, to create a frame or skeleton that is either set into the ground or mounted on concrete footings to carry the loads, roof, walls, and floor to the subgrade. Although, structurally, the poles directly in the ground will support a light structure, this system is not recommended for any permanent structure because the poles are more prone to decay. The loads are transferred by each post to the ground, becoming a series of points. Depending on the soil's bearing capacity, this form of building is limited in the load it can support. A point footing system does not have the advantage of a continuous masonry foundation, which distributes the loads over a greater surface area and is used in most permanent house or commercial construction. Although limited in the masses it can support, for most landscape structures a pole system is adequate.

The second, a timber frame system, is really an extension of the pole system. This system can be adapted to a pier, pier and beam, or continuous foot-

RELATED SPECIFICATIONS
03100 — Concrete Formwork
03200 — Concrete Reinforcement
03300 — Cast-in-Place Concrete
03370 — Concrete Curing

ing system; however, the loads in a traditional timber/beam system are transferred through the posts to the footings, not over the entire wall. In this system timbers are used for all the framing and, thus, fewer framing members are required; however, they are considerably greater in size than those used in the rib or platform system (see Figures 3.99A and B).

The third system, rib framing, also called platform framing, is common in the United States for residential and commercial wood frame construction. There are several differences between the rib and pole systems. In the rib system all perimeter and interior load-bearing walls transfer the loads in a linear fashion rather than in point fashion, distributing the loads continuously. Openings within the walls are designed so that the loads from above are transferred through "headers" to other parts of the wall. Either a continuous perimeter foundation or a pier and beam system is used in rib, or "stick frame," construction.

FOUNDATIONS

As with most landscape features built of wood, the integrity and stability of the structure, whether a pavilion, gazebo, cabin, storage shed, play structure or other exterior building, is dependent on the foundation. A failure of the structure can often be traced to this connection, where the forces of the structure are conveyed into the earth. There are several design options for building foundations and, as in deck systems, soil conditions (including depth of freeze), combined dead and live loads, structural configuration, and aesthetics all have an affect on the choice of option.

A cast-in-place pier footing is common for pole or timber framed structures built on stable soils. A pier footing is a two-part system consisting of a spread footing and a pier. The spread footing, 6 to 8 in. thick, is poured into an excavated hole, with reinforcing bars set into the pour extending vertically at a 90 degree angle from the top of the spread footing, to be incorporated into the pier. A vertical square or circular form is placed atop the reinforcing bars and secured. The spread footing, typically 6 to 8 in. wider than the pier, is sized through calculations based on soil bearing capacity and the loads supported by each post or pier (see pages 103–105 for calculating footings). It is not uncommon to extend the pier above the finished grade to receive a wood post or beam so as to avoid contact between the framing and the ground. The footing locations are determined by the structural design configuration and the allowable spans of the beams. In the design of a timber frame structure, posts are sometimes located at the midpoint of the beam. If they are nonbearing, this is of little concern; otherwise, the loads must be calculated and the beam sized to carry the post. After the piers are poured, post bases or beam seat connectors are located and set in the concrete.

A continuous cast-in-place stem wall foundation may be used if soils cannot support a pier system or if considerable loads are applied along the foundation alignment. The spread footing is a steel reinforced footing, twice the width of the stem wall or greater, 6 to 8 in. thick, and set below the maximum frost line. Any settlement of the spread footing can cause subsequent failure in the structure, and the footing must sit on undisturbed earth or earth that has been recompacted if disturbed. A series of ½ to ⅝ in. reinforcing bars are placed 8 to 12 in. OC, with a 6 in. right angle bent on the embedded end to resist withdrawing and 2 ft protruding vertically in alignment with the stem wall (see Figure 3.100). A key, or hollow depression, centered and extending the length of the spread, is created by setting an angled wood form into the pour that is removed once the concrete is set. As the stem wall is poured, the void is filled and "keyed" into the spread footing.

The stem wall form is erected using plywood or rough cut 1× material and supported by 2 × 4s called studs (vertically positioned) and wales (horizontally positioned), which are connected through the forms with snap ties. These prevent the forms from spreading and are broken off after the forms are stripped. The mechanical connectors, including anchor bolts for sills and

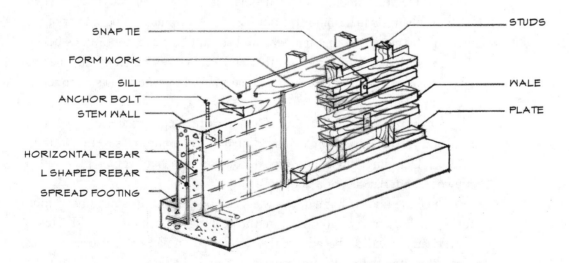

Figure 3.100   When building on a continuous foundation, the wall is formed by pouring concrete into a "false work" or wooden form. The walls consist of a reinforced spread footing and stem wall. A 2× member, a sill is bolted to the top of the stem wall upon which the wooden wall framing is attached. *Source:* Illustration by Daniel Winterbottom.

post anchors for posts, are set into the pour. Often, on foundation walls that will be seen, various details—chamfers, recessed bandings, and scored lines—are cast into the form, providing visual interest and a finished look.

The third method, employed when soils are very unstable or the foundation is very long, is called a pin pile grade beam system. This system, although very effective, is not often employed for most structures addressed by landscape architects, but should be considered in special situations. Instead of trenching for a continuous foundation, which can be expensive and requires considerable volumes of soil to be removed, a series of pilings are driven down to bearing soils or bedrock. These pilings—precast reinforced concrete, steel I beams, or reinforced cast-in-place columns—are connected to a grade beam, a long, continuous reinforced square or rectangular concrete beam. The beam is cast in place, and the name of the system refers to its placement on grade instead of being elevated as most beams are. Each of the pilings is connected through reinforcing bars stubbed out of the pier and bent at 90 degree angles parallel to the beam, and attached to the horizontal reinforcing bars used in the beam. The loads are transferred from the top of the beam down through the pin pilings to bearing soils.

Once the foundation is completed, the floor and wall framing is erected. The floor is framed in a manner similar to that described for the decking system earlier in this chapter. The beam is connected to the pier footings. If a stem wall or pier and beam foundation is used, 2 × 8 or 2 × 6 sills are bolted down on the preset anchor bolts. The joists are laid atop the sills and attached with joist hangers to a rim joist, a double 2× that frames the perimeter of the wall. In this condition the stem wall and sill function as a continuous beam. To support midspan joists, joists that end between perimeter walls, beams either spanning the perimeter walls, or supported by wood posts or concrete piers support the joist ends.

For open structures, 2 × 4 or 2 × 6 decking members are set across and attached to the joists. For enclosed structures there are several flooring options, including tongue and groove softwoods or hardwoods, plywood, a plywood underlay tile, or a floor covering.

Once the floor is framed, the walls can be erected. It is not uncommon for the wall framing to go up before the decking or sheathing is laid. This is particularly practical, because if the floor needs repair or replacement it is very difficult with the wall framing set on top of the floor materials. For most exterior structures, gazebos, picnic shelters, playhouses, saunas, greenhouses, and the like, a combination of timber and rib framing is employed, depending on the intended use and desired appearance.

WALL FRAMING

There are two primary types of wood framing for buildings. In the first, platform framing, the loads are carried by the bearing walls. The second, timber framing, incorporates a series of large posts and beams or girders to carry the loads. A potential advantage of timber framing is the wide, clear open spaces between the structural members; in the rib system, these are filled with studs (vertical framing members). Rib framing, common in the United States, is also referred to as balloon stick framing. Conceptually, a series of walls composed of many small vertical members are joined at the corners and transfer the loads to the foundation, eliminating the need for large structural posts and beams. The walls are formed on a horizontal bottom plate attached to the floor framing that establishes the alignment of the walls. Running perpendicular to the bottom plate are the studs, 2 × 4s or 2 × 6s, depending on the wall thickness, spaced 16 in. apart for a bearing wall and 24 in. for a nonbearing wall. The studs are capped with a top plate, two 2×s (see Figure 3.101). At the points where the wall is penetrated for windows and doorways, the opening is framed with two members, a king stud that frames the sides of the openings and a

Figure 3.101   Rib or platform framing is the conventional wood frame building method in the United States. The rib method uses greater amounts of material of a smaller size than the timber frame method. The loads are transferred through the walls to the foundation. *Source:* Illustration by Chad Wichers.

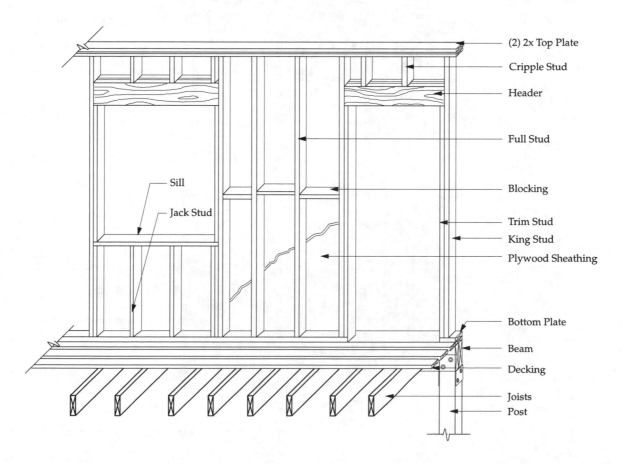

(2) 2x Top Plate
Cripple Stud
Header
Full Stud
Blocking
Trim Stud
King Stud
Plywood Sheathing
Bottom Plate
Beam
Decking
Joists
Post
Sill
Jack Stud

Figures 3.102 A–C
A. Three methods of timber framing. I. uses a continuous post with a segmented or broken beam. II. uses a continuous beam with a broken post. III. illustrates the platform or "rib" method of framing. *Source:* Ilustration by Daniel Winterbottom. B and C provide various joints commonly used in timber frame construction. *Source:* Illustration by Chad Wichers.

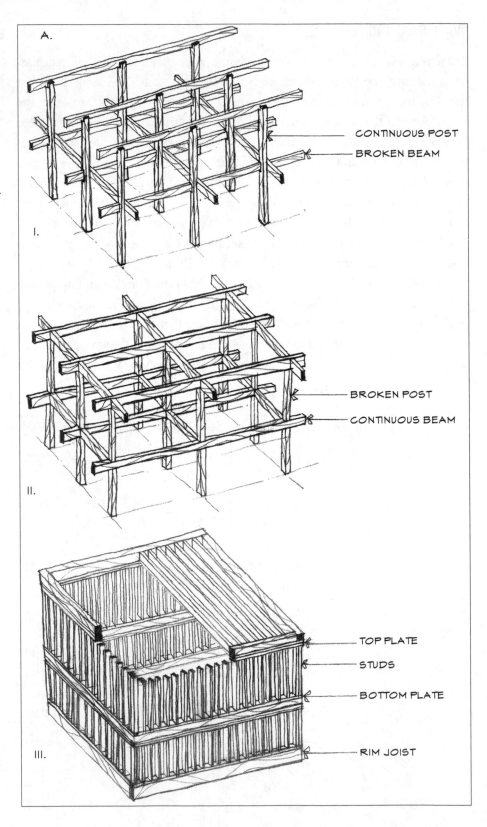

A.

I.

CONTINUOUS POST
BROKEN BEAM

II.

BROKEN POST
CONTINUOUS BEAM

III.

TOP PLATE
STUDS
BOTTOM PLATE
RIM JOIST

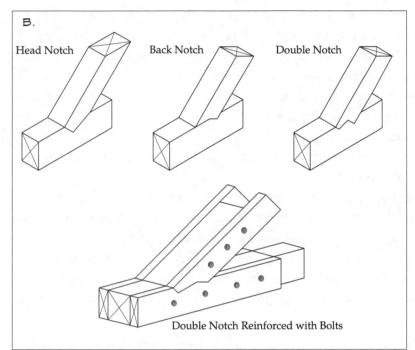

B.

Head Notch   Back Notch   Double Notch

Double Notch Reinforced with Bolts

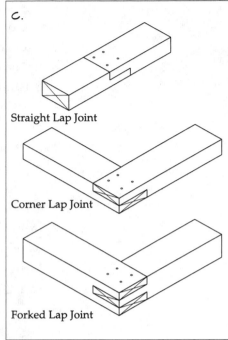

C.

Straight Lap Joint

Corner Lap Joint

Forked Lap Joint

trimmer or jack stud, attached to the king stud and cut to fit below and support the header. The header, a double 2×6, 2×8, or 2×10 member, spans the opening, transferring the loads to the king/jack studs (see Figure 3.101). The shortened framing members filling the area between the header and the top plate are cripple studs, also placed 16 in. OC. In framing a window opening, the bottom of the header defines the top dimension, and the sill caps the shortened or jack studs below the window and defines the bottom elevation of the window (see Figure 3.101). Once the framing is in place, the sheathing, often ½ in. plywood, is placed and attached to the framing and functions as shear panels (sheathing) that resist racking and lateral stresses.

Timber framing, one of the early forms of wood construction, gained prominence during the classic timber frame period, from the fourteenth century up to the eighteenth century. When the growing middle class desired "durable" masonry buildings, timber framing declined in popularity. Timber framing was revitalized in the nineteenth century and proved economically advantageous in erecting the large, open industrial structures of the time.

There are many variations of timber framing. Two versions of post and beam systems are discussed because they offer some significant advantages over rib framing. The continuous beam system (the first version) incorporates large timber or glue-laminated beams to span great distances, and the resulting clear span creates a very open structure. The spans are determined by the size of the beam and the spacing of the posts. The second system incorporates continuous posts or columns rising two stories or more. In this system the beams are connected to, rather than mounted on, each post (see Figure 3.102 A). The two systems are often combined, using split beams or split posts. In the split beam system, two members are either attached to the side of the column or set into a precut seat. In the split post method, the post is built of two or more vertical members that sandwich and mechanically connect the post to the beam.

In traditional post and beam timber construction, such as that found in early barn buildings and in the magnificent Japanese pavilions, the wood members are not attached mechanically, but are connected using a variety of wood joints, and wooden dowels and pins hold the connections together. Many joints are simple mortise and tenon, lap, or notched joints; however, variations on these forms can become very complex and ornamental (see

Figure 3.103 A small timber frame structure in New York's Central Park. Here the post supports a continuous split beam. Note that the curved brackets supporting the beam ends create an open-sided structure.

Figure 3.103). In modern timber framing many designers rely on metal connectors in lieu of complex joinery to attach wood members. The connectors often become themselves design features, as seen in the structures of Green and Green.

POST ORNAMENTATION AND TRIM

Wood as a medium for architectural ornamentation has a rich history. Many species, such as poplar, cedar, and mahogany, are easily sculpted with chisel and saw and can be painted to create graphic patterning. While Carpenter's Gothic is referred to as the heyday of effusive and elaborate embellishment in wood, all periods of American architectural style have offered opportunities for the designer to challenge the carpenter (see Figure 3.106A). Ornamentation can be found on wood structures in every region. Gingerbread pavilions in Nantucket, Massachusetts are animated with pictorial scroll work and latticed columns. The porches of summer houses in Key West, Florida have animated railings and balustrades that are lathe-turned and painted in luminous colors. In the southwestern Spanish Colonial Style vigas, brackets and carved spiraling columns are carved, and incised patterns and religious motifs are found on doors and lintels.

The proliferation of styles in the nineteenth century, High Victorian Gothic, Queen Anne, and Craftsman, corresponds to the evolution of woodworking technology and availability of skilled craftsmen. With the development of the steam-driven jig saw and lathe, mass production and new technologies were replacing the chisel as the tool for shaping wood. The mass marketing of stock components seems to have fueled the appetite for individual expression by designers and craftsmen, as witnessed by the legacy of unique and visually provocative structures in the garden, park, and domestic landscape. Through nineteenth-century pattern books, a varied selection of manufactured wood components and patterns became commercially available (see Figure 3.104D). Today the tradition still continues in both historical restoration and in contemporary design exploration.

There are a number of elements fundamental to exterior structures that lend themselves to ornamentation, such as verge boards (ornamented boards on the gable ends of structures), porch skirts (the infill boards below the porch decking), newel posts, and the repeating elements of fences and railings. How they are crafted requires the choice of the designer and craftsman. The following are some of the techniques that are commonly used (see Figures 3.104 A–D).

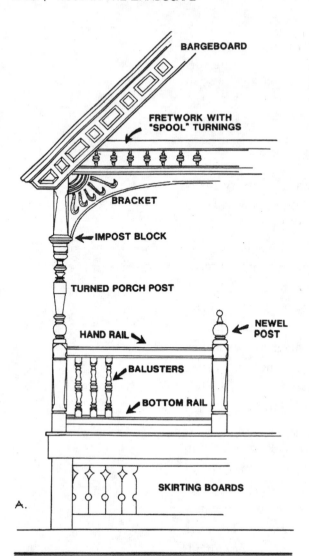

BARGEBOARD

FRETWORK WITH "SPOOL" TURNINGS

BRACKET

IMPOST BLOCK

TURNED PORCH POST

NEWEL POST

HAND RAIL

BALUSTERS

BOTTOM RAIL

SKIRTING BOARDS

A.

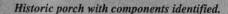

Historic porch with components identified.

B.

C.

Figures 3.104 A–D A. The primary components of the historical porch include the verge board (barge board), valance (fretwork), post, handrail, and skirt board. *Source: As Good as New,* Jakubovich, City of Milwaukee, 1993. B. A New England porch with scroll-work brackets, spindle and stick railing, and solid board skirt. In this example the skirt prohibits air circulation and should have holes or slits integrated into the design. C. A porch post illustrating scroll and appliqué work. D. A page from a 1904 Universal Design Book illustrating the stock turned and sawn balusters that were available. *Source: The Victorian Design Book,* Byrne, Lee Valley Tools, 1984.

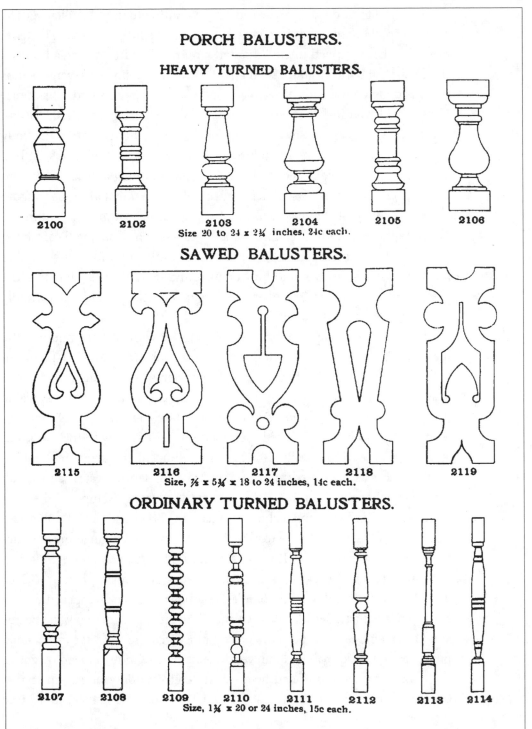

PORCH BALUSTERS.

HEAVY TURNED BALUSTERS.

2100   2102   2103   2104   2105   2106

Size 20 to 24 x 2¼ inches, 24c each.

SAWED BALUSTERS.

2115   2116   2117   2118   2119

Size, ⅞ x 5¼ x 18 to 24 inches, 14c each.

ORDINARY TURNED BALUSTERS.

2107   2108   2109   2110   2111   2112   2113   2114

Size, 1¾ x 20 or 24 inches, 15c each.

D.

Holes, slits, and slots are formed by saw-cutting to transform flat vertical or horizontal boards into ornamental patterns of solid and void. The technique has been applied to create patterns on porch skirts (the area between the decking and the ground), solid board fences, gates, brackets, verge boards (boards defining the ends of a gabled roof), and in the gable ends of summer houses and pavilions beneath the ridge beam (see Figures 3.104 A and 3.106 A). The voids are sawn into the sides of, or centered within the body of, the boards which when assembled create a repeating pattern. This method is often combined with other techniques such as carving and scroll-work to create a combination of sculpted and graphic ornamentation (see Figure 3.104 A). Many of the historical motifs derive from natural and anthropomorphic imagery. In this technique the holes—often of square, heart, club, feather, leaf, or flower shapes—are combined with slits and slots symbolizing stems, stalks, arrows, and human anatomy. Slits can be as thin as a saw blade while slots are wider and are predominantly straight, although with jig saws curved forms are possible.

Scroll-sawn ornamentation became popular with the invention of the mechanized band saw, allowing the commercial production of flat-sawn balusters, brackets, gable-end ornaments, and verge boards, all of which were available from suppliers during the nineteenth century and are still available through specialty restoration supply houses (see Figures 3.104 B and D). Many designers have developed their own forms, and as with the holes and slots, many are symbolically derived. In addition to the above mentioned, scroll work was also used to create appliqué for fences, gates, and porch skirts. The Victorian Gothic gazebos represent a classic example of the integration of technologies and techniques including holes and slots, scroll-sawn, pediments, finials, and lattice work to create a transparent gingerbread structure as an ornamental tour de force (see Figures 3.105 and 3.106 A).

The process of stick-work uses thin pieces of lumber, often 1 × 2 or 2 × 2, to create simple and complex compositions. They appear in gable ends, fence balustrades, or porch valances (an area framed below the beams and spanning between the posts or columns) that are used for ornamental purposes. To create patterns the wood pieces are set in rectilinear, diagonal, or "crazy" (pieces positioned at many different random angles) patterns. Common forms include sunbursts, diagonals, grids, and constellations (see Figure 3.105).

Through this "Chinese" bandstand, a sense of the exotic was brought to mid-western America. The columns appear translucent through the scale of the posts and the use of infill diagonal stick work. The scroll-sawn extended eaves are reflective of Chinese pavilions, and the dental work on the valence provides a seamless transition between the columns and the roof. The whole composition, crowned with the cupola and finial, reflects the "playful" approach to detailing. *Source:* From *Decorating Eden,* edited by Elizabeth Wilkinson and Marjorie Henderson © 1992. Published by Chronicle Books, San Francisco. Used with permisssion.

A.

B.

Figures 3.106 A and B   A. The Dairy, in New York's Central Park, is an example of the High Victorian Gothic designed by Calvert Vaux, Fredrick Olmsted's partner at the time. B. An example of contemporary scroll-sawn bracket design in the Central Park children's zoo in New York City.

Spindlework is commonly found in porch balustrades, valances, and gable ends. Spindles are wood members that have been turned on a lathe or assembled from components creating lineal sculpted pieces. A selection of spindles and actual porch designs featuring the use of spindles in balustrades and valances can be found in nineteenth-century pattern books. The spindles, once installed, can be elaborately painted so that each part of the spindle becomes a color feature or can be finished with a uniform color, featuring its shaded forms as a pattern (see Figure 3.104 A, B, and D).

The shaping of wood by carving is one of the oldest forms of decorated wood, and the use of a chisel is not dependent on later technological innovations such as the band saw. Because carving is labor intensive, it became restricted to one-of-a-kind items such as gargoyles, masks, and heraldry, and in the elaborate carved gable ends rendered in the sunburst design. This form of ornamentation became lost once mass production of scroll-sawn spindles, brackets, and columns became widely available.

Appliqué of wood shapes is a combination of scroll-sawn flat work set on a solid board backing. The result is a raised scroll-work that differs from the character of the transparent silhouetted forms of traditional scroll-work. The use of appliqué can be found on columns and brackets, gable ends, verge boards, on pediments above porches, and on solid board fences and gates. The scroll cut elements are mechanically attached or glued to the backing boards and are often accentuated through the use of contrasting colors (see Figure 3.104 C).

In addition to gazebos, pavilions, and kiosks, the most elaborate use of exterior wood ornamentation is found on porches. The porch evolved from what was originally called a verandah or portico into what has become the ubiquitous uncovered deck, popular only in the last thirty to forty years. During the nineteenth century the porch was a highly articulated element of the house and a primary link between the structure and landscape (see Figure 3.104 A–D). The covered porch supported by columns, with railings defining the floor area and the pitched gable roofs lent itself to extensive ornamentation (see Figure 3.104 C). Porches, bandshells, raised gazebos, and other exterior structures are often enclosed from the floor framing to the ground plane with open lattice work or sawn-slat skirting boards (see Figure 3.104 A and B). Whatever the choice, the skirt should have adequate penetrations to facilitate air circulation so moisture doesn't build up and cause decay to the posts or floor framing. The skirting can be designed as a striking ornamental focal point with patterns cut into the vertical edges, and holes and slots cut into the plank boards can be designed to create complex patterns.

Stairs in exterior structures present ornamental opportunities in the detailing of rails, balustrades, and newel posts. The railing for the stairs typically matches the railing surrounding the flooring, and limitless options can be created using heavy or thin turned or sawn balusters. The stair railing, often terminated at the bottom tread with a newel post, is made of either solid or boxed materials. The shaft in a turned post is often ornamented with rounded shapes, and the rectilinear posts are detailed with raised moldings or carved or routed flutings. The newel post is typically designed to be matched with porch columns and balustrade spindles in an effort to create a harmonic whole.

The column in most structures represents one of the primary focal points, and the range of styles include the standard classical columns and caps (Doric, Corinthian, Tuscan, and Ionic, etc.), as well as the porch-style columns. The latter may be turned, chamfered, and fluted to be incorporated into the design and accented through the use of color (see Figure 3.104 A).

Brackets are used on porches to serve as visual connections between the columns and the valance, fretwork, or beams. The range of brackets as presented in the nineteenth century pattern books is impressive. Brackets are formed with a 90 degree angle top and side to fit between the column and horizontal plane. The angle formed by the tangent is either angled, curved, rounded, or scrolled. Brackets can incorporate pendants, spindles, holes, slots, and appliqué in their designs. The brackets are often visually prominent and in some situations represent the most elaborate detail within the overall structure (see Figures 3.104 B and C and 3.106 A and B).

The valance (fretwork) is the last detail before the roof. The valance runs vertically between the beam and bracket, and horizontally between the columns. The infill is composed of solid boards, spindles, stick-work, or scroll-work. In many cases it duplicates the balustrade forms while in others it differs. In both it serves to link the porch or lower architectural expression to the upper floors or to the roof detailing (see Figures 3.104 A and 3.109).

ROOF FRAMING

After the walls are erected, the roof framing can begin. There is a plethora of potential roof configurations; most are designed with either rafters or trusses

Figure 3.107   Roof framing of a WPA structure in Camp Long, Seattle. The rafters supported by large beams meet at the ridge beam, forming the peak. The cross ties provide bracing for the rafters.

or some combination of these. The framing of a flat roof is relatively simple and quite similar to joist framing. Most roofs on small exterior structures are designed with a slope or a combination of many slopes. A single sloped roof, called a shed roof, is the simplest, connecting two walls of differing heights. A double sloped roof, or hip roof, uses walls of the same height to support the lower ends and a ridge beam to support the rafters at the peak (see Figure 3.107). Beyond these basic forms many variations can be found, including multiple-hipped roofs, domed roofs, octagonal roofs, and butterfly roofs (see Figure 3.108). Whatever the configuration, there will have to be rafters or trusses to support the dead and live loads. In northern climates, snow can add considerable dead loads over long periods and the rafters will have to be of great size (see Figure 3.109). In southern climates snow is not a concern, but wind uplift can cause great stresses and the anchoring of the rafters must be thorough. In conventional framing the rafters bear on the top plate, or in timber framing on the beams, and in a simple hip roof the rafters run to the ridge, where they are connected to and bear upon a ridge beam. The ridge beam is a $2\times$ or greater material running parallel to the walls, to which rafters

Figure 3.108   Note that all rafters are straight members as illustrated by this bell roof of a band pavilion in Randolph, Vermont. The rafters are formed from a series of 2× members jointed and cut to form a compound curve. Note the board sheathing supporting the roofing material. Randolph, VT.

Figure 3.109   A pole frame bell-shaped roof structure (Randolph, Vermont). The roof cladding, asphalt shingles, provides a degree of flexibility appropriate for covering curved surfaces.

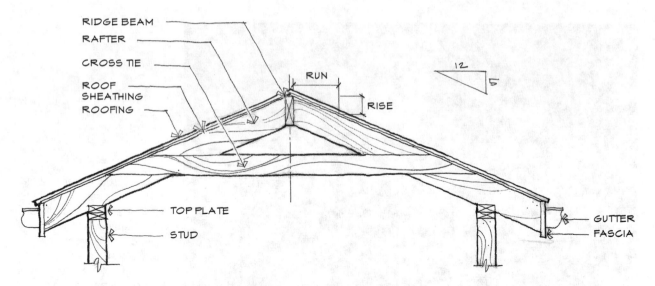

RIDGE BEAM
RAFTER
CROSS TIE
ROOF
SHEATHING
ROOFING
RUN
RISE
12
5
TOP PLATE
STUD
GUTTER
FASCIA

Figure 3.110   The roof, sheathing, and roofing material is supported by rafters. The angle of the rafters determines the pitch of the roof. The pitch is designated by rise over run, and as illustrated in this diagram, the ratio or pitch is 5:12. Where the rafters meet the top plate a notched cut or "bird's mouth" is created to allow the rafter to sit on top of the plate. *Source:* Illustration by Jody Estes.

are attached. The pitch (slope or angle) of the roof rafters is established by the relationship of the rise (vertical distance) to run (horizontal distance). Thus, a 5.12 pitch indicates that for every 12 in. of horizontal run the rafter rises 5 in. (see Figure 3.110).

Often, a wood member referred to as a collar tie, placed at the midpoint of the span, is used to tie the rafters together and to increase resistance to sagging and spreading. On large projects it is common to use premanufactured forms of rafters set at the specified pitches, called trusses, which are delivered to the project, hoisted up, and set on top of the walls to form the roof line. Trusses designed with multiple bracing can span large distances and are employed when long, clear spans are required, such as for large gathering halls and covered bridges.

ROOFING

With the roof framing completed, the sheathing, most commonly ½ to ¾ in. plywood or 1 × 6 skip sheathing, is used to tie all the rafters together and to provide a substrata to attach the roofing material to. The sheathing is covered with overlapping sheets of roofing (tar) paper before the final roof cladding system is attached, so as to provide protection from water penetration. There are many roofing systems available on the market—durability, cost, and aesthetics will determine the final selection. For most landscape structures, insulation value and roof venting are not of concern; the roof cladding is intended to shed water, complement the character of the structure, and resist wind and snow loads. The options for impermeable roofs include, but are not limited to, asphalt, cedar and slate shingles, metal sheet systems, and terra-cotta tiles (see Figure 3.109). Some systems require extra nailing supports and may be substantial in size to carry the weight of slate or terra-cotta tiles. The costs and durability vary, depending on the method selected. The roof cladding is attached with roofing nails, screws, or other systems that are provided by the manufacturer. Some sheet systems are interlocking and attached to the sheathing with clips; others use galvanized roofing nails under overlapping singles to protect the points of penetration. A system of ring-shanked nails combined with rubber washers are used where surface nailing is exposed. Copper-coated nails, designed to prevent galvanic corrosion, are available for fastening copper roofing. The roof conveys water, and a structure such as a gutter is installed to route the water to a downspout system. Alternatively, the rafter tails can be extended beyond the building face to shed the water away from the siding. If the function is solely to provide shade, the roof may be designed as a permeable system, providing screening from the sun and as an armature for vines (see Figures 3.87 and 3.93, pages 129 and 133). Wood, bamboo, or metal members span the rafters, creating an open pattern which can be seen in the shadows cast on the floor. Roofs can also be extended past the walls to create overhangs and reduce the angle of sun penetration into the structure.

As mentioned previously, roofs offer many opportunities for ornamentation including the patterning of the shingles themselves. There are four common wood elements that lend themselves to ornamentation, including finials and cupolas, barge boards and rafter tails, brackets, and gable ends (see Figure 3.105, page 151). Finials are used to celebrate the termination of the hip roof and are found in many forms, including linear saw-cut, scroll-work pieces, to solid-turned urn and rounded shapes. Flat saw-cut fleur de lis pieces are found on the gable ends of nineteenth-century structures in the northeastern United States and carved pineapples, urns, and conical forms crowning gazebos, bandstands, and pavilions can be found in both Europe and in the United States from the sixteenth century on. The cupola serves both an ornamental and functional purpose. In an enclosed louvered structure the louvered cupola serves as a ventilator, allowing heat and fumes to circulate up and out of the structure. The form often takes on the characteristics of an oversized finial, highly articulated and frequently crowned with an actual finial at the peak. They were and are used in pavilions, gazebos, and summer houses, more as an ornamental feature than as a functional element. The forms vary from octagonal bell shapes to rectilinear structures with hip roofs. Examples can be found with up-turned rafter ends crowning Chinese bandstands (see Figure 3.105, page 151).

The forms found in gabled roof structures of summer houses, gazebos, bandstands, and pavilions lend themselves to two common types of ornamentation: verge boards (barge boards) and rafter tails and gable ornaments (see Figures 3.104 A and 3.106 A, pages 148 and 151). Gable ornaments are essentially infill decorative elements situated beneath the ridge line or peak of the gable that provide visual interest and serve no structural function. They are most often integrated into a verge board pattern, but can be found on structures with nondescript trim or verge boards. The gable ornaments are most common in Victorian Gothic and Queen Anne architecture, although examples can be found in simple cottages as well. There is a wide range of elements and methods used in the application of gable ornaments, including scroll-sawn, spindlewood (often in sunbursts), pediments, stick, appliqué, and carved (often sunbursts); many of these methods are often used together. Verge boards, by creating shadow patterns, celebrate the gable end which is often the entry face of the structure. The patterns are often created by stickwork, scroll-sawn, and carved patterns with pediments and brackets. As mentioned above, flat or rounded finials often extend up from the peak, crowning the gable end. Rafters may extend beyond the eaves in Craftsman style structures, and their ends or tails may be sawn into decorative forms.

RELATED SPECIFICATIONS

06050—Fasteners and Adhesives

06100—Rough Carpentry

06200—Finish Carpentry

06400—Architectural Woodwork

07300—Shingles and Roofing Tiles

07400—Manufactured Roofing and Siding

07600—Flashing and Sheet Metal

07700—Roof Specialties and Accessories

BRIDGES

Since early man first laid down a felled tree limb to cross a stream, wooden members have been used to construct a variety of timber bridge structures. In many parts of the country the timber bridge has become an icon, expressing the character and culture of the region. The covered bridges of New England are treasured historic structures, and the railroad trestle bridges of the Northwest continue to evoke the days of towering forests of trees of enormous girth (see Figure 3.113). Although the depletion of these resources may, in hindsight, be questioned, the ingenuity and daring to assemble these structures contributes to our American mythology. Timber construction has

Figure 3.113   In the United States the iconic timber wooden bridge is a recognizable image of timber craft and engineering. Designed to shed snow, receive light, and span great lengths, these structures represent the rural New England culture of resourcefulness, simplicity, and integration with the land. Woodstock, Vermont.

changed over the centuries and is no longer a prevailing building method, but many clients and designers are choosing to incorporate timber bridges in their projects and parklands. A contributing factor has been the development of new technologies to fabricate the structures at reduced cost and with longer serviceable life.

Timber bridge construction has evolved over thousands of years, from a single log spanning a waterway, to railroad trestle and covered bridges, to the glue-laminated structures used today. It is believed that inspiration for the early wood suspension bridges came from hanging vines in tropical areas, which were later used to lash the members together. Although there are no records, historians speculate that pontoon bridges made of lashed timbers were used to span rivers in military campaigns by the Persians, Chinese, Greeks, and Romans. The oldest record of a stationary bridge is a reference to a bridge crossing the Tiber River in Rome in 621 B.C. that used a wooden superstructure to span stone buttresses. A Trojan bridge across the Danube River reportedly rested on 20 timber piers, 150 ft high and 170 ft apart. The supporting wood piers were impregnated with oils and resins to prevent deterioration. The development of timber bridges in Europe reached a high level of mastery in the late eighteenth century with the use of deck-stiffening raked frames and built-up timber arches. Although covered bridges were not the norm, they were occasionally built to increase longevity and serviceability. The Schaffhausen Bridge spanning the Rhine River and the Chapel Bridge at Lucerne, constructed by the Grubenmann brothers, are notable examples.

Outstanding timber bridges in Asia include the Kintai Bridge, dating to the seventeenth century in Japan. It consists of a series of arched coffered beams that are supported by stone piers, creating a rhythmical sequencing as the pedestrian travels along the arched walkway.

The early bridges in the United States were "pioneer bridges" with short spans, or trestle bridges for longer spans, with closely spaced piers, built by the new settlers landing along the New England coast. In 1785 the first timber bridge to span a multiple beam length was constructed in Bellows Falls, Vermont. The structure spanned 365 ft with a natural rock pier for midspan support (Ritter, 1990, 1–6). Although the covered bridge has become a symbol of the New England landscape, the first covered bridge was in fact built in 1804 across the Schuylkill River in Philadelphia.

Construction and innovation with timber grew with the proliferation of rail lines and highways. Iron fasteners were incorporated into the structure to connect standardized members. The distinctly American covered bridge, designed for increased longevity, was in great demand. "An estimated 10,000 covered bridges were built in the United States between 1805 and 1885." (Ritter, 1990, 1–8).

The development of pressure preservative treatments in 1865 enabled the building of bridges without covering. By the end of the nineteenth century steel became the preferred material for bridge construction, although timber structures continued to be built. By the mid-1930s it was cheaper to construct a steel bridge, and wood was relegated to the decking. It was also during this period that reinforced concrete became a commonly used material for deck construction, and with the advent of prestressed concrete, entire bridges were made of cement.

In the 1940s a major technological innovation brought timber back as a competitive bridge building material. Glue-laminated members, relatively lightweight, cost competitive, and able to span great distances, became the

Figure 3.114   Most contemporary timber bridges are fabricated from glue-laminated members, which are cost-effective and allow a variety of forms. This bow trestle pedestrian bridge in Woodenville, Washington, recalls the railroad heritage of the West.

primary material for timber bridge construction. In the 1980s stress-laminated members were introduced, further expanding the construction of timber bridges (see Figure 3.114).

SUBSTRUCTURE AND SUPERSTRUCTURE

A timber bridge is essentially a two-part system. The supporting structural system, the substructure, carries the dead weight of the superstructure and the live load of the traffic across it. The second system, the superstructure, spans the distance between the supports and transfers the live load to the substructure.

Substructure

The substructure is composed of a number of elements. *Abutments* are located at each end of the bridge, support the load at each end, and retain the earth at the approaches to the bridge. There are a number of abutment types ranging in cost and application (see Figures 3.115 A–D):

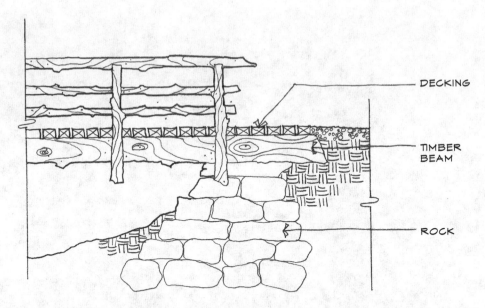

DECKING

TIMBER
BEAM

ROCK

A. ROCK ABUTMENT

Figures 3.115 A–D
Illustration by Daniel
Winterbottom.

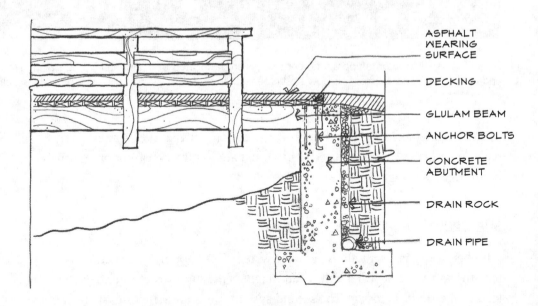

ASPHALT
WEARING
SURFACE

DECKING

GLULAM BEAM

ANCHOR BOLTS

CONCRETE
ABUTMENT

DRAIN ROCK

DRAIN PIPE

C. CONCRETE ABUTMENT

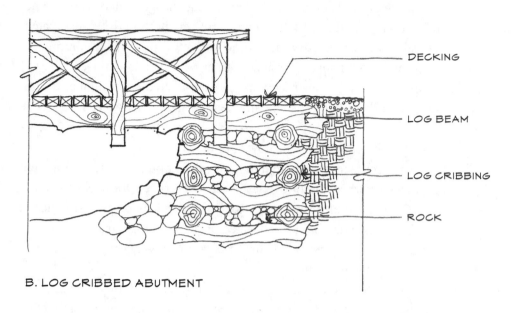

DECKING

LOG BEAM

LOG CRIBBING

ROCK

B. LOG CRIBBED ABUTMENT

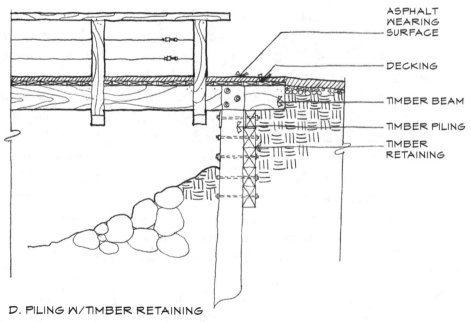

ASPHALT
WEARING
SURFACE

DECKING

TIMBER BEAM

TIMBER PILING

TIMBER
RETAINING

D. PILING W/TIMBER RETAINING

1. Simple abutments are characterized by low cost and simplicity. They rely on a stable ground support and a low-profile bridge design. They are not anchored below the frost level, and movement should be anticipated. Typical examples are dry laid stone and multiple-sill log abutments. These are used for small crossings with culvert-type log bridges.

2. A spread footing is constructed of pressure-treated sawn lumber or glulam placed directly on the embankment surface. This system must have stable material to support the loads without settlement, scour (undermining of the channel by the flows), or erosion.

3. Cribbing abutments are common when the approaches are at different elevations or when the bridge level has to be raised for adequate water flow. Cribs are preferably constructed of cedar logs or precast concrete members. The crib should be located away from the stream channel so that it is not susceptible to scour. Cribs are relatively easy to build from locally available materials.

4. Post abutments are timber posts attached to a spread footing below the ground surface. These are used to elevate the superstructure and to retain the approaches with back and wing walls.

5. Timber or precast concrete pile abutments are used if the abutments are in the water course, the bank is too steep for cribbing, or the soil is too soft to support footings. The superstructure is attached to a continuous cap of sawn or glulam members that are fastened to the piles. These abutments typically contain back and wing walls to retain the embankment.

6. Piers, or bents, are intermediate supports between abutments. They are built of log piers or sawn lumber frames. They can be used when the foundation material is suitable and the height does not exceed the available material. The base must be below scour level, and the piers or bents are often sited on small islands or rock outcrops. They should be as narrow as possible to minimize obstruction of stream flow. Frame bents are used when the foundation material is not suitable for piers or for higher elevations.

7. Concrete foundations and abutments range from low pads on stable foundation material, to support sills for stringers, to concrete abutments with wing walls retaining the embankment. These abutments are the most expensive to build and endure the greatest impacts with the longest life span.

Figure 3.116   Posts, beams, and decking form this pedestrian bridge at the Blodell Reserve, Bainbridge Island, Washington. Note the size of the decking and the flashing above the post and bracket, typical of the plank and beam method of construction. *Source:* Photo by William MacElroy.

Superstructure

The substructure provides the support for the superstructure. There are five basic types of superstructures, including beam, laminated slab, truss, trestle, and suspension.

The longitudinal beam is the simplest and most common type of superstructure. The decking is supported on a series of timber beams that span two or more supports. The beams are either stringers or, for greater strength, girders. The beams are constructed of a variety of wood members (see Figure 3.116). Untreated logs are commonly used for temporary structures with an average lifetime of 10 to 20 years on low-volume roads. Spans of 20 to 60 ft are common, although spans of a 100 ft are possible. The use of sawn lumber is limited by the availability of members of an appropriate size, usually 4 to 8 in. by 12 to 18 in. The members are generally found in spans of 15 to 30 ft, with solid blocking between the beams for lateral support. Examples of this form of superstructure can be found throughout the United States and, with restoration, date back to the eighteenth century. Sawn members have an average life span of 40 years when treated but are now being replaced by glulam beams. Glulams can span greater distances than timbers, and because of their large sizes, fewer beams may be required. A span of 20 ft to 80 ft is common, and glulam beams have spanned distances of 140 ft. The length of the beams is usually restricted by access or transportation to the construction site.

A new type of structural composite material, laminated veneer lumber, is being considered for bridge construction. The product is being developed and tested by the U.S. Department of Agriculture (USDA) Forest Service, Forest Products Laboratory, and its use may increase in the future.

Glulam or nail-laminated sawn lumber slab or longitudinal deck structures are designed to span distances of approximately 40 ft without supporting members or beams. The low profile of the structure and the economical benefits are applicable for many projects. The lumber used varies from 2 × 8s to timbers 4 in. wide and 16 in. deep.

If there is adequate height or the crossing is particularly deep, and substructure costs are high, a glulam deck arch bridge is an effective option. The aesthetic can be very powerful, creating a strong portal through a deep embankment.

Other common forms of superstructures use trusses, usually including two main trusses, bracing, and a floor system. In bridge construction the bowstring (or parallel-chord) truss is most common. In a bowstring truss the top chord is arched with either curved glulam members or a series of straight sawn members. The bowstring is economical for spans up to 100 ft, and through-trusses or deck-trusses are used for spans up to 250 ft. The expense of truss fabrication and installation is high, and because of its many members and joint connections, this structure can be costly to maintain. Most of the timber truss bridges built today are chosen on the basis of their aesthetics.

One of the oldest forms of bridge construction relies on trestles, a series of beam, deck, or truss superstructures supported on timber bents (Ritter, 1990, 1–8). Trestle bridges make longer spans feasible, and many of the old railroad bridges are of this type. Their use has declined since the 1950s, with the development of glulams that extend span capabilities.

Rarely used for vehicular traffic, but found in pedestrian applications, are suspension bridges. They are particularly efficient for very long spans (more than 500 ft) when intermediate supports are not possible. Cables connected to vertical timber structures support the decking.

The final element of a superstructure is the decking that serves to distribute the live loads of the vehicular or pedestrian traffic to the supporting members of the structure (see Figure 3.116). The deck material is usually either sawn lumber planks, "nail-laminated lumber," or glulams. "Sawn lumber nail-laminated" decks are usually 2 in. thick timbers with the flat side vertical. The planks are nailed together to form a continuous surface. With the introduction of the glulams the nail-laminated decks have declined in popularity. The oldest form of decking is sawn lumber planks, laid flat, perpendicular to the beams. The planks range from 3 to 6 in. in thickness and are spiked to the supporting members. This form of decking does not protect the structure, and the deck deflection makes asphalt paving impractical. This form is restricted to low-volume or pedestrian bridges.

A glulam deck is constructed of panels ranging from $5\frac{1}{8}$ to 9 in. thick and 3 to 5 ft wide. They are laid perpendicular or in a longitudinal orientation to the beams. The deck is constructed as either an interconnected or doweled surface. A doweled surface uses steel dowels to connect the panels, and although more expensive than the interconnected system, it can produce a thinner decking and better performance with an asphalt wearing course. The glulam protects the substructure from water, increasing the longevity of the structure.

A new method, termed the stress-laminated timber process, uses vertical sawn lumber that is clamped together on the wide face with high-strength stressing rods. This method is used primarily in longitudinal decks. The process is also used in restoring nail-laminated decks where delamination has occurred. The system functions in a manner similar to glulam decks.

PRESERVATIVES

See "Wood Preservative Treatments," page 41, in Chapter 2.

CONNECTORS

Mechanical fasteners easily join wood in two basic connections: lateral (shear) connections and withdrawal (tension) connections. A variety of types of fasteners are used in bridge construction, depending on the application. With the exception of the timber connectors, which include split rings and shear plates held together with a lag or through bolt, the connectors are fairly common. The simplest are spikes or nails, and their use is limited to nonstructural applications such as laminating decks. They are more susceptible to withdrawal caused by vibration or dimensional change in the wood. The most common fasteners are bolts, used for moderately high-strength lateral connections and in tension connections. Lag screws are also incorporated in bridge construction, especially where one side of the structure has limited access. Drift pins and bolts are used to connect heavy timbers and are inserted into predrilled holes. The bolts have a head for use with steel side plates. In addition to these stock fasteners, custom-fabricated connection plates and cable connectors for suspension bridges are incorporated where needed (see Figure 3.117). All metal connectors should be galvanized for corrosion protection and can be colored with a high-grade exterior finish if desired.

COSTS

The costs for timber bridge construction and installation vary, depending on the type of construction, type of materials and preservative used, and constraints on access to the site.

Figure 3.117   This custom-designed connector ties members together at different angles—creating a harmonious marriage of steel and wood.

Figure 3.118 A rusticated balustrade combined with a rough-hewn timber frame structure spans a small creek in Central Park. The use of wood and the intentional rural vernacular creates a wonderful surprise, located in the middle of New York City.

Figure 3.119 As true for a bridge post as it is for a fence post, the end grain is susceptible to moisture infiltration. At the Japanese Garden in the Brooklyn Botanical Garden, a traditional form of copper post cap is employed on the bridge post.

Studies conducted on vehicular timber bridge construction from 1989 through 1993 show that costs for bridges in areas where softwood species are readily available are lower than those in regions were hardwoods predominate. It was also shown that bridges using standardized lumber had a cost advantage over those requiring customized items. The average 1994 cost was $47.20 per square foot of superstructure. Costs were highest in the mid-Atlantic area and lowest in the Pacific Northwest. A cost comparison of species showed red maple being the most expensive and red pine the cheapest (Timber Bridge Information Resource Center, May 1994). Costs were also affected by the length of the bridge, with a trend indicating that longer spans reflected higher costs.

Costs for pedestrian bridges also increase with longer spans. As explained by Chris Rodgers of Bowbends, a manufacturer of custom bridges, the "increased length dictates the thickness and depth of the girder, which will drive the unit costs higher." Pedestrian bridges are often more stylized, reflecting specific periods or vernaculars, and the detailing required typically affects the costs (see Figure 3.118).

For small pedestrian projects, prefabricated bridge kits are available from a number of suppliers (e.g., Bowbends and D. F. Magnum Co.). These bridges tend to have short spans and are usually for residential, recreation, or short-span park purposes. There are a few companies that have a standard line of steel structure with timber decking and rails (e.g., Steadfast and Contental). These bridges have longer spans and are sized for vehicular, equestrian, and pedestrian uses. A third category includes the companies that specialize in glue-laminated timber bridges that include long and short span applications. These companies have some standard designs, but more commonly work with designers to customize the standard designs to fit the requirements of a particular project (e.g., Western Wood Structures, Cedar Forest Product Companies, and Unadilla Laminated Products). See Figure 3.119.

The landscape architect specifies the bridge locations on the site plan and either proceeds with construction documents for the bridge or, alternatively, contacts a bridge contractor/fabricator. The engineering of large timber bridges has become highly specialized, and many landscape architects and architects have not acquired the expertise to design them. The industry has recognized these difficulties, and a procedure, called bidder-design, has been created by Michael Ritter, structural engineer, formerly with the USDA Forest Service. The concept allows the designer to reduce engineering costs by enlarging the project parameters to include the design, based on American

Association of State Highway and Transportation Officials (AASHTO) specifications, with qualified materials to be used by the selected contractor. The landscape architect gives the contractor specifications including spans, width, loading, foundation type, railing, wearing surface and design parameters. The process then becomes one of collaboration between the landscape architect and the selected contractor to finalize the construction documents.

In 1989, Congress funded the formation of the National Timber Bridge Initiative through the USDA Forest Service, with the appointment of Stephen C. Quintata, program director of the National Timber Bridge Information Resource Center. The initiative addressed economies devastated by cutbacks in the logging and wood-related industries. The intent is twofold. The first goal is to research the feasibility of using native woods in timber bridge construction to create economical bridge systems, expand the markets for wood products, and improve rural transportation networks. The second goal is to change the current perception among many engineers and designers, to convince them that timber can provide a viable alternative to other bridge materials. Timber is currently perceived to be limited to low-volume short-span rural roads where aesthetics are a major consideration. To date, the initiative has funded 289 bridges in 48 states and 30 pedestrian timber bridges. In addition to the demonstration projects, the National Forest Service has constructed approximately 300 wood bridges in the National Forest System.

RELATED SPECIFICATIONS

03100	Concrete Formwork
03200	Concrete Reinforcement
03300	Cast-in-Place Concrete
03370	Concrete Curing
06050	Fasteners and Adhesives
06100	Rough Carpentry
06130	Heavy Timber Construction
06170	Prefabricated Structural Wood
06200	Finish Carpentry
06300	Wood Treatment

APPENDIX A

ALTERNATIVE MATERIALS AND SUSTAINABLE
METHODS OF WOOD PRODUCT PRODUCTION

New building products and processes are developing, spurred on by a growing understanding of the environmental stresses resulting from the unmitigated extraction of timber resources (see Figure A.1). A profile of a sustainable design ethic is emerging with such wood-related concerns as reducing waste, using recycled materials, choosing the least toxic preservatives and finishes, and supporting environmentally responsible practices in timber production and harvesting. Sympathetic designers and clients will find a widening arena of choices and interests to balance. A few journals,

Figure A.1   As with any decking, the orientation, dictated by framing placement, becomes the patterning. Here a plastic lumber composite radiused decking forms a hexagonal pattern. Adopt-a-Park, University of Washington Design/Build Studio. Instructors Luanne Smith and Daniel Winterbottom, 1999.

most notably *Environmental Building News,* provide up-to-date information on new products and test data on those that have been submitted to American Society for Testing and Materials (ASTM) standards. There are also many local and regional publications and state and federal resources for "green" products and methods for their use in design and construction.

Probably the simplest and most direct way designers can affect the environment is to consider their designs in terms of waste creation. Of the solid waste generated in the United States and Canada, 10 to 30% is derived from construction and demolition combined. The chief material in this waste stream is woody material, including solid sawn lumber and manufactured wood products (plywood, engineered lumber, pressure-treated lumber, etc.) Although recyclers are using the generated waste for fuel, composition products, and lumber substitutes, and sewer sludge for mulching and bulking agents, the best practice is to reduce the amount produced. Before construction begins, designers should specify materials of standard size and dimension the members so that any cuts can be reused within the project. For example, the floor joists of a deck can be dimensioned so that the end cuts can be reused for blocking. This is especially valuable for treated wood members, as their use as recycled material is very limited and they become both wood and chemical waste when discarded.

CERTIFIED LUMBER

The certification of forest operations and wood products is a very new and slowly developing field. The intent is to engage a certified forest manager, preferably someone independent of the wood products industry, to evaluate and certify that the wood in question comes from a responsible, well-managed operation. There are a number of certifying bodies in the United States and a number in Europe as well. The first certifying program in the world was the SmartWood program. Founded in 1989 as a nonprofit program of the Rainforest alliance, an environmental watchdog group, it was followed in this endeavor by the Scientific Certification Program (SCS), a private for-profit company. SmartWood and SCS are the only two certifying bodies in the United States, and each has its own set of criteria. In order to achieve standardization, the Forest Stewardship Council (FSC) was founded in Toronto in 1993. The FSC has adopted and revised its Principles and Criteria, "which has become the uniform standard that affiliated third party forest certification organizations now follow" (Wilson, 1997, 1).

In 1997, 1.6 million acres of forest in the United States had been certified, and this number is expected to double. However, that represents only one-third of 1% of public and private timberland in the country. The evaluation of forestry practices can be achieved through field audits, but responsibility through the milling operations may be more difficult. On visual inspection the difference between certified and noncertified lumber is indistinguishable; thus, tracking is critical.

The American Forest and Paper Association (AF&PA), representing about 90% of the industrial timber companies, has its own Sustainable Forestry Initiative. Participants follow a mandatory set of forestry guidelines and file annual reports demonstrating their compliance. The process does not include independent field verification.

The Canadian system examines and certifies not the wood products, but the companies that produce them. The Canadian Standards Association (CSA) standards are designed to improve environmental stewardship in forest management. Participating producers set goals and targets for implementing sustainable practices, and once accepted by the stakeholders, these bind the company. In this process there is no labeling of products as in the FSC's certification, but when they are registered, the companies assure that their forest management goals and methods are ecologically based and that extraction and harvesting are done in a sustainable manner.

Although these certification systems vary in approach, they are not much different in practice. They both provide interaction with certification reviewers and give foresters an outside view to better understand their own operations and process flows, and how they can become more sustainable.

An advantage of the FSC forest certification system is that the forest resource managers are certified, rather than the tract of land. This system enables the product from many small plots under the supervision of a certified manager to be certified, which, given the cost of certifying forest lands, would not be possible in a land-based certification process. Until 1997 all lands certified were private holdings; a number of state and county lands are being reviewed.

Producers of certified wood products face a challenging marketplace. Current FSC regulations provide that products containing 70% certified wood can carry the certification label. A reduction from 100% was deemed necessary in order to put more material into the mainstream market.

The Certified Forest Products Council, in Beaverton, Oregon, actively promotes responsible forest product buying practices throughout North America. It remains uncertain as to whether consumers will join its efforts by paying the higher cost of certified wood at the lumberyard. The CSA approach of certifying an operation may prove more successful in promoting product acceptance than the FSC's costly chain-of-custody–based certification system.

LUMBER SUBSTITUTES

Plastic lumber manufactured from recycled plastic products has been available since the early 1990s. The acknowledged father of the technology in the United States is Floyd Hammer, founder of Hammer Recycled Plastics, Inc. Many companies, both large and small, are in the market, improving the product and lowering its cost as the technology continues to advance.

Plastic lumber can be grouped in several categories, utilizing different plastics and manufacturing processes and varying in composition, quality consistency, properties, and performance. Plastic lumber is an integrally col-

Figure A.2   Benches have become a product easily fabricated from plastic lumber.

ored board product requiring no coatings and absorbing no moisture (see Figure A.2). It does not rot, splinter, or peel, thus requiring substantially less maintenance than wood lumber products. The dimensions of plastic lumber are consistent with those of wood dimensions — 1× material is actually ¾ in., 2× is 1½ in. However, recent tests have shown that many of the samples were not uniform in profile as a result of inconsistent shrinkage in the manufacturing process, and some of the samples were bowed (Sachan, Nosker, and Renfree, 1994). In addition to the standard dimensional lumber, many manufacturers produce custom lumber in special profiles and thicknesses. Although plastic lumber has many virtues and may be a substitute for wood in certain applications, it is not necessarily a replacement. Some manufacturers are incorporating the lumber with steel reinforcing, but testing is needed to evaluate the differential in material expansion rates. Its structural use is limited by the size of the members required. Plastic has a flex modulus of three to four times that of wood, increasing with higher temperatures. The addition of glass fibers to increase the rigidity of the lumber has proved promising in recent tests. In designing plastic lumber structures, supporting members should be spaced closer than normally spaced with wood to mitigate bouncing or sagging. Many manufacturers recommend spans of 12 to 14 in. for decking (see Figure A.3). A representative of Durawood has suggested "a 15 in. span for supporting members for a 2× in. thickness of the decking under typical loads." Another producer, Envirowood, Inc., recommended, "A piece of plastic lumber with a thickness of 1½ in. should be supported 10½ in. on center to give equivalent deflections as that of a 1½ in. thick piece of wood placed 16 in. on center." All spans and bracing should be calculated for the specific type of material used in designing structures to ensure structural integrity and prevent sagging of deck members. The contraction and expansion rate is greater for plastic lumber than for wood. Rates should be checked with the manufacturer and adjustments made to the specifications. For example, an 8 ft beam of Durawood may expand or contract ¼ in. over a 50°F temperature change.

Plastic lumber is considerably heavier than wood of the same dimensions. A 2 × 4 manufactured by the Plastic Lumber Company weighs 1.8 lbs per linear foot (lf). The same product, as distributed by Earth-Wise Supply Company, weighs 2.2 lbs per lf. This is compared with a weight of 1.2 lb per lf for pressure-treated lumber and 1.2 lb per lf for pine 2 × 4s. Plastic lumber weights differ among manufacturers, and products using foaming agents are significantly lighter than solid products.

Figure A.3   This wood/wood scrap composite product provides good traction on this ADA accessible ramp. The Garden of Eat'in, University of Washington Design/Build Studio. Instructors Luanne Smith and Daniel Winterbottom, 1998.

MANUFACTURING

Producers use a variety of the plastics found in packaging and industrial waste to manufacture plastic lumber. An understanding of plastic lumber includes an understanding plastics terminology. The following are the common plastics used in the manufacture of plastic lumber.

> *Polyethylene,* often referred to as PE, comes in the form of high-density PE (HDPE) and low-density PE (LDPE). Examples of HDPE include milk and detergent bottles, and LDPE includes bags, film, and wrapping material.
>
> *Polyethylene terephalate,* also known as PET, is found in soda bottles and household containers.
>
> *Polypropylene,* or PP, is common in bottles with special filling requirements, such as ketchup bottles, and in plastic parts that require considerable "memory."

Polyvinylchloride, commonly referred to as PVC, is found in cooking oil bottles, some mineral water bottles, and blister packs.

Polystyrene, or PS, is commonly found in expanded foam coffee cups and service ware such as utensils.

These plastics are recycled into the following commonly available types of plastic lumber:

1. Purified plastic lumber (such as Durawood and Duratech) utilizes a single post-consumer plastic, such as HDPE. The raw product is collected from residential or industrial bins, sorted, ground into a flake, and processed in a wash-dry system to remove any impurities. The flakes are heated, and the resulting resin is compounded with pigments. The melted material is then extruded or molded into a rigid board stack material, the finished product having approximately 90% recycled content by weight. At least two manufacturers are producing a lumber with a lighter foam core and a denser integral skin on the outer face. The weight is reduced by approximately a third of that of a comparable solid product.

2. Commingled recycled plastic lumber (Hammer's, Envirowood, and Earth Care products) are generally lower in cost and are made with two or more plastics. As with purified plastic lumber, the raw materials are ground, cleaned and melted, and usually either extruded or extrusion-flow molded into a board product. Because different types of plastics are used, there may be variability in the physical properties of the board, making specification for some uses difficult. Different plastics can vary in their tolerances to chemicals and stresses. Research to improve quality is ongoing.

3. A third method, the composite process, is used to create a nonpure plastic lumber product (Lifecycle, Trimax (with glass fiber reinforcing), Tirbrex, Trex, and AERT). The material is manufactured by adding composite materials to the plastic resins. A typical mix is approximately 50% PE (primarily LDPE) and 50% sawdust or other secondary fiber. These products tend to be stiffer than pure plastic lumber and to have rougher textures. Because of the fiber content, these products have been shown to absorb up to 8% moisture in a 24-hour period, which restricts their use in certain applications. Coatings may have to be applied for insect resistance and color retention.

Producers of all types of plastic lumber have to remove all impurities in the manufacturing process. In compression tests, contaminants such as oils can affect the bonding of the matrix mix, causing potential fracture points in the product. A consistent cell structure is important to maintain predictable tensile and compression properties and to ensure uniform integrity and density. Air pockets or voids in the cell structure can also affect the process and success of mechanical fasteners.

INSTALLATION

Plastic lumber can be cut and fabricated with traditional woodworking tools, including power saws, drills, and so forth (see Figure A.3). Nails and staples can be used, but temperature expansion can loosen joints; mechanical fasteners such as bolts or deep-flight screws (drywall screws) are recommended for attachment. Predrilling is not necessary for screws. Some manufacturers supply a clip system for deck installation. Plastic lumber is very difficult to glue, and most manufacturers do not recommend it. There are heat fusion welding techniques under experimentation, but most plastic lumbers are polyethylene based and thus exude a waxy material to the surface, making adhesion very difficult. Experiments are being conducted with welding equipment and processes, which may introduce new fastening techniques.

COLORS

Color in plastic lumber is achieved with the incorporation of specific pigments that have chemical bonds that provide stabilization under radiant energy loads. Special ultraviolet (UV) graded pigments that decrease fading over the years are available. Although the UV additives can improve color retention, certain pigments are prone to fading. In general, grays, black, and the earth tones are more colorfast. It is important to note that the concentrated pigments used are designed to disperse in specific plastics at varying temperatures. The adding of coloring resins to lumber formed from differing plastics must be monitored to ensure color mating and retention.

Most manufacturers create a textured product, often mimicking a wood grain, that increases the product's skid resistance. The pattern is imbedded into the product as it is cooling in a malleable state. In general, pure HDPE products tend to be smoother than commingled products. Similarly, continuous extruded products are smoother than those produced with the molded process.

Plastic lumber is graffiti-resistant. A high-pressured wash will remove most paints, and marks created with marking pens can be removed with turpentine. A slight shadow may appear, which can be buffed off with sandpaper. Shallow carvings can be eliminated with a hot iron.

COSTS

Plastic lumber costs (in 1999) are, on average, two to three times those of pine lumber and are comparable with those of redwood. Plastic lumber made from purified HDPE with a foamed core is at the high end in price. The commingled products are generally less expensive. A commingled product manufactured by Envirowood lists at $.76 per lf in black and at $1.00 for colors. In general, these costs are coming down with improved manufacturing processes and increased competition. Are these products worth the added cost? Their life span is virtually infinite; the fasteners will probably fail before the plastic does. In addition, the products contain no preservatives that can leach and contaminate the surrounding ground or water. The high-quality products are exceptionally resistant to moisture, corrosive substances, insects, and environmental stresses. Plastic lumber is virtually maintenance free, requiring no waterproofing, painting, or staining.

The greatest limitations to the use and specification of plastic lumber has been a lack of uniform testing procedures and standards. As of 1997, the ASTM has approved test methods for compressive properties (D-6108-97), flexural properties (D-6109-97), density and gravity (D-6111-97), creep (D-6112-97), and for mechanical fasteners (D-6117-97). ASTM is continuing work to develop additional standards and specifications.

As costs decrease, quality improves, and standards are developed, plastic lumber holds promise for use in a variety of applications, from marine to gardening, where longevity and prevention of contamination by leachates are of concern.

NONTOXIC AND LOW VOC FINISHES

Most paints on the market contain volatile organic compounds (VOC), which are chemicals used in the finishes as binders or carriers that give off gases and can be inhaled, affecting the user's health. For users, there are two reasons to avoid VOCs in paints. The first is to protect the ambient air quality, and the second is to maintain the indoor air quality when paints are used in an enclosed structure. When exposed to sunlight, VOCs create "ground-level ozone, a pollutant and smog (that aggravate) respiratory problems, damage plants, and contribute to global warming" (Malin, 1999, 12). The reduction of ground-level VOCs is the primary motivation behind recent regional, state, and national regulations limiting the amount of VOCs in finishes. The second effect of VOCs, on indoor air quality, is not caused by sunlight, inasmuch as this is often filtered or screened, but there is a concern that potential health effects can result as VOCs react with other chemicals in the coating and in the air. In addition to VOCs, there may be other indicators of paint toxicity; however, to date the results of research remain inconclusive. For more information, see *Environmental Building News,* February, 1999.

There are many available film coatings that are marketed as "low-odor," "zero-VOC," and "very low VOC"; however, it is very difficult to eliminate VOC emissions entirely. One problem is that the testing of off-gasses loses accuracy at very low levels, and some products labeled "zero-VOC" may not be entirely free of VOCs. The common coloring and tinting agents contribute significant amounts of VOCs; thus, lighter colors or those brands using solvent-free coloring agents will reduce VOC emissions.

There are several coatings advertised as low-toxic paints that contain solvents chosen for their low toxicity levels; others contain chemicals derived from plants or use binders such as milk to avoid petrochemicals altogether. Many of these alternative paints perform differently from traditional paints, with coverage ability reduced, and with the absence of biocides, they are more susceptible to mildew spread. The "natural paints," mostly European imports, use plant-based resins, solvents, and pigments, or milk proteins or casein; however, as compared with petro-based products they can be tricky to work with and often demand skilled craftsmen to apply them successfully. Although the natural paints may not contain petroleum-based solvents, they may cause toxic reactions among chemically sensitive users because some of the natural VOCs can react to the ozone in the air to form formaldehyde.

There is also a growing interest, particularly in public agencies, in using recycled paint for economical and environmental reasons. Some agencies provide such products free to the public, and a few manufacturers are offering recycled exterior paints for sale on a special-order basis. In most cases the color range in recycled paints is limited to neutral colors.

In selecting "green" paints, the following guidelines should be considered:

- Choose paints with the lowest VOC levels possible.
- Buy paints from companies that actively recycle or sponsor paint collection programs.
- Choose paints that have a certified seal by an ecological labeling group, such as Green Seal.
- Check Material Safety Data Sheets (MSDS) available from the manufacturer to determine potential health effects.
- Calculate needs to avoid overordering. Calculators designed for paint surface estimating are available.

APPENDIX

SPECIFICATION STANDARDS

Prior to 1963 there was no accepted standard for specifications of building materials or methods, and form and language varied widely among practitioners. To address this inconsistency, the Construction Specifications Institute (CSI) with the American Institute of Architects (AIA) developed an industry-wide specification system that has become known as the MasterFormat "uniform system." MasterFormat organizes detailed construction information into a standardized order, or sequence, on the basis of products and methods. The system has been adopted by many of the building industry and professional associations, including the American Society of Landscape Architects (ASLA). The written specifications are one component of the construction documents, which consist of a project manual (bidding requirements, contract forms, conditions of contract,) the specifications, and the drawings. During the construction process addenda and contract modifications will be added. Thus, the specifications complement the drawings and other documentation to provide the contractor a complete and binding description of what is to be built and where it is to be located.

The MasterFormat system consists of 16 divisions, sequentially numbered, each representing a work unit, (e.g, Doors and Windows, Division 8), a material (e.g., Concrete, Division 3), or a construction system (e.g., Site Work, Division 1). The divisions are further broken down into *broad scope* sections, which carry a five-digit numerical designation based on the section. For example, Division 6, Wood and Plastic, is composed of the broad scope sections (e.g., 06100: Rough Carpentry; 06130: Heavy Timber Construction; 06159: Trestles; 06170: Prefabricated Structural Wood). The broad scope sections always follow the sequence set out by the uniform system. If a section is not used, the sequencing remains. The broad scope sections are further broken down into *medium* and *narrow scope* sections. These are specific work units that are more limited in scope, which can be grouped under the broad scope section. For example, under Division 6, Wood and Plastics, is a broad section numbered 06100 and entitled "Rough Carpentry." Within this section are the narrow scope sections; for instance, number 06125 is "Wood Decking." The concept is to nest narrow scope sections into broad scope sections and into the 16 divisions, all within that nesting being related by subject and numerical designation. This nested classification scheme helps to organize communications on large projects involving many workers, managers, and designers.

Each narrow scope section is organized into three parts. Part 1, titled "General," contains a description of the administrative, procedural, and temporary requirements unique to this specific section. General administrative and procedural information applying to the entire job is found in Division 1 at the beginning of the documents. Part 2, "Products," describes the materials, products, equipment, systems or assemblies that are to be incorporated into the project. This part also specifies the quality standards of the materials to be used. Part 3, "Execution," describes the preparatory actions and methods by which the products are to be incorporated into the project. Site-built assemblies and manufactured products and systems are included (see Appendix C).

A format for division, section, and page can be obtained either electronically or in paper format through Masterspec.

APPENDIX  C

SAMPLE SECTION ORGANIZATION

PART 1 GENERAL

1.01. Section Includes (Content description)

1.02 Allowances (Range of acceptability)

1.03 System Description

1.04 Submittals

    A. Shop Drawings (Details supplied by the fabricator)

        1.

        2.

    B. Product Data (Available from the manufacturer)

        1.

        2.

1.05 Quality Assurance (Quality standards to be met)

1.06 Environmental Requirements

1.07 Warranty

1.08 Maintenance

PART 2 PRODUCTS

2.01 Material or Products

2.02 Components or Configuration

2.03 Accessories

2.04 Mixes

2.05 Fabrication (Description of methods)

2.06 Shop Finishing (Description of methods)

PART 3 EXECUTION

3.01   Examination and Preparation

3.02   Installation and/or Application and/or Erection (Description of methods)

3.03   Erection Tolerances (Field standards)

3.04   Schedules

Adapted from MASTERSPEC® User's Guide, Copyright 1988 ARCOM.

APPENDIX

RELEVANT ORGANIZATIONS AND AGENCIES

AF&PA
American Forest and Paper Association
1111 Nineteenth Street NW, #800
Washington, DC 20036
202-463-2700

ALSC
American Lumber Standard Committee
P.O. Box 210
Germantown, MD 20875-0210
301-972-1700

ASTM
American Society for Testing and Materials
100 Bar Harbor Drive
West Conshohocker, PA 19428
610-832-9721

AWPA
American Wood Preservers Association
P.O. Box 286
Woodstock, MD 21163-0286
410-465-3160

FPS
Forest Products Society
2801 Marshall Court
Madison, WI 53705
608-231-1361

USDA
National Timber Bridge Information Resource Center,
Northeastern Area
180 Canfield Street
Morgantown, WV 26505
(304) 291-1591

USDA
U.S. Department of Agriculture
Forest Service
Forest Products Laboratory
One Gillford Pinochet Drive
Madison, WI 53705-2398
608-231-9200

SFPA
Southern Forest Products Association
P.O. Box 641700
Kenner, LA 70064-1700
504-443-4464

WCLIB
West Coast Lumber Inspection Bureau
P.O. Box 23145
Tigard, OR 97281
503-639-0651

WRCLA
Western Red Cedar Lumber Association
1200-555 Burrard Street
Vancouver, BC V7X 1S7
Canada
604-684-0266

WWPA
Western Wood Products Association
522 SW Fifth Avenue
Portland, OR 97204-2122
503-224-3930

CRA/RIS
California Redwood Association/Redwood
Inspection Service
405 Enfrente Drive, Suite 200
Novato, CA 94949
415-362-0662

GLOSSARY

Adhesive   A liquid or semiliquid material used to bind two or more pieces of wood together.

Ammoniacal copper quat (ACQ)   A waterborne wood preservative containing copper, quat salt, and ammonia. For specifications see American Wood Preservers Association (AWPA) standards P-5.

Ammoniacal copper zinc arsenate (ACZA)   A waterborne wood preservative containing copper, zinc, and arsenic. For specifications see AWPA standards P-5.

Annual growth ring   The layer of growth during a single growing season. The rings can be seen in cross-sectional cut, with each ring representing a year's growth.

Appearance grade   Boards ¾ in. and thicker; 2 in. and wider are selected for visual appearance.

Arbor   A wood skeleton used to support climbing plants. An arbor typically has four posts, whereas a pergola has a series of posts, creating a continuous linear structure.

ASTM   American Society for Testing and Materials

Balustrade   A row of balusters, vertical fence, deck, or stair railing members that span between the bottom and top rails.

Beam   A horizontal structural member that rests on or is attached to a post or column. A beam transfers the loads from the joists or plank decking to the posts.

Blocking   A short wood member placed between two vertical or horizontal members to increase rigidity or provide a platform for attachment.

Bolt   A steel or stainless steel mechanical fastener used to attach one wood member to another. Requires a predrilled hole through which the shaft of the bolt is placed. A nut is screwed onto the end securing the two pieces together. See *lag screws* for further information.

Bow   A bend in a single curve of a wood member along the length of its plane.

Bracing   Wood members used to counter the tendency of an elevated structure to rack or roll over.

Butt joint   A joint where two nonoverlapping wood members abut each other end grain to end grain.

Cantilever   A member projecting beyond a single bearing point at one end.

Cap   A wood member designed to sit atop another and project just beyond its face, as in a post cap that covers the end grain of a post, or a rail cap that covers a rail. A cap can be shaped to provide ornamental interest and/or a useful platform.

Cedar   A species of wood noted for its durability, having natural chemicals that resist deterioration. Red cedar is common in the Northwest, white cedar in the Northeast, and Alaskan cedar in Alaska.

Chamfer   An angle cut into the longitudinal edge of a wood member.

Check   A separation within a wood member that extends across annual growth rings, often the result of rapid dying.

Chromated copper arsenate (CCA)   A waterborne wood preservative containing chromium, copper, and arsenic. For specifications see AWPA standards P-5.

Connector   A fastener, commonly fabricated out of metal, used to join two or more pieces of wood.

Countersink   A hole drilled in wood and made to position the end of a bolt and its nut and washer.

Cross grain   The grain parallel with the widest dimension and perpendicular to the narrowest dimension of a board.

Cup   A warpage in a board that causes a curving that deviates from a straight line across the width of the board.

Dead load   The combined weight of all permanent nonmovable members.

Dead man   A wood member extending perpendicularly back from the face of a timber wall. The dead man, anchored to the wall and into the soil, provides resistance to overturning.

Decking   Wood boards laid perpendicular to a joist or beam, which transfer the live and dead loads to the structural members below and provide a walkable surface for the users.

Dimension lumber   Lumber with a nominal thickness of 2 to 5 in. and a nominal width of 2 in. or greater. Available as stress-graded lumber with design values for structural use.

Dovetail   A type of wood joint with a flaring tenon and a mortise into which it fits, creating an interlocking joint.

Dowel A wood or steel cylindrical pin that fits into predrilled holes between abutting members to prevent motion. Used to attach finials to post caps, in timber framing, and in timber bridge construction.

Earlywood The part of the growth ring that is formed during the early part of the growing season and is less dense and weaker that latewood. Often referred to as *springwood.*

End nail A nail driven into the end grain of a wood member.

Fasteners A family of objects designed to connect or hold wood members together, including nails, screws, bolts, and specialty fasteners.

Finial A wood object, often carved or turned to create an ornamental form. A finial is attached to the top of a post or post cap.

Flat grained Lumber that has been sawn parallel to the pith and approximately tangent to the growth rings.

Footing A continuous or individual concrete or wood form that transfers the loads from a structure to the subgrade.

Framing The structural or infill wood members used to construct a wood structure.

Freestanding A deck or other structure that is self-supporting and unattached to any other structure.

Fungicide A family of chemicals that are toxic to fungi and used to prevent fungi from forming on wood. The EPA must approve these chemicals for sale or use.

Glue laminated member (glulam) Individual wood members (laminations) bonded together with structural adhesives to create a larger wood member.

Grade stamp An official identification indicating grading agency, sawmill, grade, species, and moisture content during manufacturing that is applied to wood.

Ground contact A term describing the use of a wood member that is in contact with or submerged in the ground.

Heartwood The wood extending from the pith to the sapwood. This wood may contain extractives, gums, and resins that make it darker and more decay resistant than sapwood.

Hot-dipped galvanizing A process of single, double, or triple dipping of a fastener into molten zinc.

Incising Small perforations on the surface of the wood, left by small blades, that allow a preservative treatment to penetrate into the body of the member. Used on species resistant to natural penetration and absorption.

Joist A wood member that spans between two beams or between a beam and a ledger. Joists transfer the loads from the decking to the beams.

Kiln-dried after treatment (KDAT)   Lumber that has been kiln-dried to specific moisture contents after preservative treatment.

Knot   The remaining portion of a branch or limb that remains in the board after it is milled. Knots can fall out after the board has been dried and weaken the structural integrity of the board.

Lag screw   An over-sized screw with a threaded shank and hexagonal head on one end used to screw large wood members together when access for through-bolting is not possible.

Laminate   To bond together with adhesives two or more wood members, creating a larger member.

Lap joint   Laying two wood members cut so that when one is set on top of another to form a joint the surfaces are flush.

Lateral load   A force pushing on the vertical members that can cause a structure to rack or overturn.

Latewood   The portion of the annual growth ring formed after the early-wood has ceased developing. Referred to as *summerwood*, latewood is often denser and mechanically stronger than earlywood.

Lineal foot   A longitudinal measurement of 12 in. in length.

Live load   The combined forces of all movable objects, including animals, humans, furniture, and so forth.

Load   A pressure, either "dead" or "live," that is supported by a structure.

Longitudinal   Pertains to the longest direction, generally parallel to the direction of the wood fibers.

Lumber grade   A designation based on the use of the piece of lumber— for example, standard, utility, structural.

Mildew   A black fungus that grows on the surface of wood, causing the wood to darken over time.

Mildewcide   A chemical, added to many preservatives and coatings, that is toxic to mildew fungi.

Miter   A angled cut at the end of a wood member.

Moisture content   The amount of water contained in wood and expressed as the percentage of the weight of the wood after drying.

Nail   A steel or stainless steel fastener that mechanically attaches one wood member to another. Steel nails intended for exterior use are protected from corrosion with resistant coatings.

Penetrating finish   A finish that penetrates the surface of wood without forming a film.

Pergola   A lineal, skeletal wood structure consisting of posts, beams, and cross members. Used to provide shade or support plants.

Pitch   The accumulation of resins from a tree that may be emitted from the wood with rising ambient temperatures.

Plug   A piece of wooden dowel, glued into a depression to cover a counter-sunk fastener. The dowel is set or sanded flush with the surface of the member.

Post   A vertical member supporting and transferring the loads from the structure above to the footing or ground below.

Preservative   A chemical designed to protect wood from decay.

Pressure treatment   The application of a chemical treatment under pressure in a contained environment, increasing the penetration into a wood member.

Rafter   A member spanning the distance between exterior walls or between an exterior wall and a ridge beam that supports the roof.

Rail (stringer)   A horizontal member spanning two posts used to support either pickets, balustrades, or fence boards. Used in fences and on deck/porch railing systems.

Railing   The combination of rails, posts, and other vertical members used to define edges or facilitate movement.

Retention   A measure of the amount of preservative injected into the standard outer zone of a wood member.

Rim joist   Also referred to as a *band* or *header joist*. Two 2× joist members used to frame the perimeter of a structure to support floor decking or perimeter walls.

Sapwood   The lighter-colored wood closest to the outer part of the tree. The sapwood is more prone to decay than the heartwood.

Semitransparent stain   A penetrating preservative that contains pigmentation, protecting a wood surface against degradation from ultraviolet light.

Shear   A type of pressure applied in opposite directions, which can sever a connector or supported member.

Sister   The attaching of one member to another member running in a parallel direction with mechanical fasteners.

Splice   To unite by lapping two ends together or applying a piece that overlaps and connects the two ends.

Square foot   A square foot unit of measure; thus, a 2 × 12 at 12 in. and a 2 × 6 at 24 in. both equal a square foot.

Stain   A darkening of a wood surface caused by bacteria or by a pigmented finish used to prevent decay and ultraviolet degradation.

Treated lumber   Lumber that has been treated with an approved preservative, following standards set by the American Wood Preservers Association (AWPA) or the American Society for Testing and Materials (ASTM).

Treatment standards   Standards set by the AWPA or the ASTM that designate acceptable chemicals, retentions, and penetrations for various species and wood products.

Toe nail   A nail driven through the end of a wood member at an angle into another wood member.

Trellis   A vertical structure created with thin strips of wood.

Tributary load   The area of a deck used to calculate the loads carried by a structural member.

Turnbuckle   A threaded metal connector that can be tightened to increase tension.

Uplift   The tendency for wood members to lift up; usually caused by wind.

Varnish   A clear, film-forming finish that contains a water-repellent finish.

Water-repellent finish   A finish that contains only a water-repellent chemical.

Water-repellent preservative (WRP)   A finish that contains both mildewcides and a water-repellent chemical.

Weathering   The surface degradation of a wood member caused by ultraviolet radiation, water, or abrasion.

REFERENCES

Adams, W. *The French Garden 1500–1800*. New York: George Braziller, 1979.

Amburgey, T. "Wood-Destroying Fungi." *Fine Homebuilding* (Feb./Mar. 1992).

American Wood Systems. *Gluelams in Residential Construction*. Tacoma, WA: American Wood Systems, 1993.

AITC 109-98. *Standard for Preservative Treatment of Structural Glued Laminated Timber*. Englewood, CO: American Institute of Timber Construction, 1998.

Bring, M., and J. Wayembergh. *Japanese Gardens: Design and Meaning*. New York: McGraw-Hill, 1981.

Boerner, A. "Footbridge." *Landscape Architecture* (July 1931).

Chatfield, J. *The Classic Italian Garden,* New York: Rizzoli, 1991.

Clarke, G. "Driveway Lighting Installation," *Landscape Architecture* (July 1931).

Dufort, R. "Painting Exteriors." *Fine Homebuilding* (Aug./Sept. 1990)

Falk, B., and S. Williams. "Details for a Lasting Deck." *Fine Homebuilding* (April/May 1996).

Grove, S. "Deck Design." *Fine Homebuilding* (Oct./Nov. 1985).

Goetz, K., D. Hoor, K. Mohler, and J. Natterer. *Timber Design and Construction Sourcebook*. New York: McGraw-Hill, 1989.

Harris, C., and N. Dines. *Time-Saver Standards for Landscape Architecture*. New York: McGraw-Hill, 1988.

Herbertson, S. "Builder's Adhesives." *Fine Homebuilding* (Feb./Mar. 1991).

Ireton, K. "Concrete and Masonry Fasteners." *Fine Homebuilding* (Aug./Sept. 1987).

Ireton, K., ed. *Porches, Decks and Outbuildings*. Newtown, CT: Taunton Press, 1997.

Jakubovich, P. *As Good as New*. Milwaukee, WI: Department of City Development, 1993.

Jewel, L. "Notes on A. D. Taylor." *Landscape Architecture* 2 (1985).

Karp, B. *Victorian Ornamental Carpentry*. Mineola, NY: Dover Publications, 1981.

Malin, N. "Paint the Room Green." *Environmental Building News* 8 (2) (Feb. 1999).

McBride, S. *Landscaping with Wood*. Newtown, CT: Taunton Press, 1999.

McBride, S. "Railing Against the Elements." *Fine Homebuilding* (Oct./Nov. 1991).

McBride, S. "Building a Timber Retaining Wall." *Fine Homebuilding* (June/July 1999).

McDonald, K., R. Falk, R. S. Williams, and J. Winandy. *Wood Decks, Materials, Construction and Finishing.* Madison, WI: Forest Products Society, 1996.

Missell, R. "A Deck Built to Last." *Fine Homebuilding* (April/May 1988).

Nash, G. "Building a Picket Fence." *Fine Homebuilding* (April/May 1987).

Nash, G. *Wooden Fences.* Newtown, CT: Taunton Press, 1999.

National Timber Bridge Initiative (May 1994).

Powell, C. "A Rail-and-Stile Garden Gate." *Fine Homebuilding* (Feb./Mar. 1996).

Ritter, M. *Timber Bridges: Design, Construction, Inspection, and Maintenance.* Washington, D.C.: USDA Forest Service, 1990.

Robinson, D., D. Rosen, and A. Jaroslow. "Rustic Shelter." *Fine Homebuilding* (June/July 1984).

Sachan, R. S., T. J. Nosker, and R. W. Renfree, *Development of Standardized Test Methods for Recycled Plastic Lumber.* New Brunswick, NJ: Rutgers University Center for Plastics Recycling Research, 1994.

Sewall, S., and D. Stenstrom. "Rebuilding a Federal-Period Fence." *Fine Homebuilding* (Jan./Feb. 1985).

Schuttner, S. *Building and Designing Decks.* Newtown, CT: Taunton Press, 1993.

Schuttner, S. "Deck Foundations That Last." *Fine Homebuilding* (Feb./Mar. 1993).

Spring, P. "Stud Wall Framing," *Fine Homebuilding* (Aug./Sept. 1984).

Smulski, S. "Preservative-Treated Wood." *Fine Homebuilding* (Oct./Nov. 1990).

Smulski, S. "Lumber Grade Stamps." *Fine Homebuilding* (June/July 1996).

Tatum, G. *Landscape Gardening and Rural Architecture of A. J. Downing.* New York: Dover Publications, 1991.

Tishler, W. *American Landscape Architecture.* Washington, D.C.: Preservation Press, 1989.

Vaughan, R. "A Decorative Post Cap." *Fine Homebuilding* (Oct./Nov. 1989).

Western Wood Products Association. *Western Woods Use Book.* Portland, OR: Western Wood Products Association, 1973.

Williams, S., M. Knaebe, and W. Feist. "Why Exterior Finishes Fail." *Fine Homebuilding* (July 1997).

Wilson, A., and N. Malin. "Wood Products Certification: A Progress Report." *Environmental Building News* 6: 10 (1997).

INDEX